I0820617

LIVING OUR FAITH DAY BY DAY

Nothing will be impossible for God. —Lk 1:37

LIVING OUR FAITH DAY BY DAY

MINUTE MEDITATIONS FOR EVERY DAY CONTAINING A SCRIPTURAL READING, INSPIRATIONAL QUOTE, REFLECTION, AND PRAYER BASED ON THE NICENE CREED

By

Most Rev. Arthur J. Serratelli
S.T.D., S.S.L., D.D.

CATHOLIC BOOK PUBLISHING CORP.
New Jersey

CONTENTS

NIHIL OBSTAT: Rev. T. Kevin Corcoran, MA., S.T.B.
Censor Librorum

IMPRIMATUR: ✠ David M. O'Connell, C.M., J.C.D., D.D.
Bishop of Trenton

March 19, 2025

(T-143)

ISBN 978-1-958237-85-4

Printed in China 25 HA 1

catholicbookpublishing.com

INTRODUCTION

Even before the New Testament was written, Christians expressed their faith with short creeds proclaiming the Risen Jesus as Lord, e.g., 1 Cor 15:3-6 and Rom 10:9. In the generations following the Apostles, the Church began to produce longer creeds to insure that all believers were united in the confession of one and the same faith.

The Nicene Creed continues to be one of the most influential means not only to express the Catholic faith in its integrity but also to pass it on from one generation to the next. Our faith is the foundation of our living in Christ. On Sundays and Solemnities, we recite the creed at the very center of the Mass. It unites us as one people in one faith and serves as a guide for our living. In the following pages, we will unpack the richness of each phrase of the Nicene Creed to help us not only better understand our faith but also live courageously what we believe.

The Nicene Creed

I BELIEVE in in one God,
the Father almighty,
I believe in one Lord Jesus Christ,
the Only Begotten Son of God,
born of the Father before all ages.
God from God, Light from Light,

true God from true God,
begotten, not made, consubstantial with the Father;
through him all things were made.
For us men and for our salvation
he came down from heaven,
and by the Holy Spirit was incarnate of the Virgin Mary,
and became man.

For our sake he was crucified under Pontius Pilate,
he suffered death and was buried,
and rose again on the third day
in accordance with the Scriptures.
He ascended into heaven
and is seated at the right hand of the Father.
He will come again in glory
to judge the living and the dead
and his kingdom will have no end.

I believe in the Holy Spirit, the Lord, the giver of life,
who proceeds from the Father and the Son,
who with the Father and the Son is adored and glorified,
who has spoken through the prophets.

I believe in one, holy, catholic and apostolic Church.
I confess one Baptism for the forgiveness of sins
and I look forward to the resurrection of the dead
and the life of the world to come. Amen.

VERY moment in life is an act of faith.

—Paulo Coelho

JAN. 1

I believe...

REFLECTION. We cannot go through life without saying in one way or another, "I believe." We need to trust others.

We believe what scientists tell us of the universe, what doctors tell us of medicine, and what historians tell us of the past. We choose to believe and trust what the Church teaches us of God.

PRAYER. *Lord, help me believe, even when I do not understand.*

DO NOT seek to understand in order that I may believe, but I believe in order to understand.

—St. Anselm

JAN. 2

I believe...

REFLECTION. By saying "I believe," I acknowledge my own inability to grasp all reality with absolute certitude. I question. I doubt. I do not fully understand.

Yet, faith opens a door for me to understand the world as meaningful and purposeful and allows me to live even with doubts.

PRAYER. *Lord, lead me beyond my doubts to faith in You at all times.*

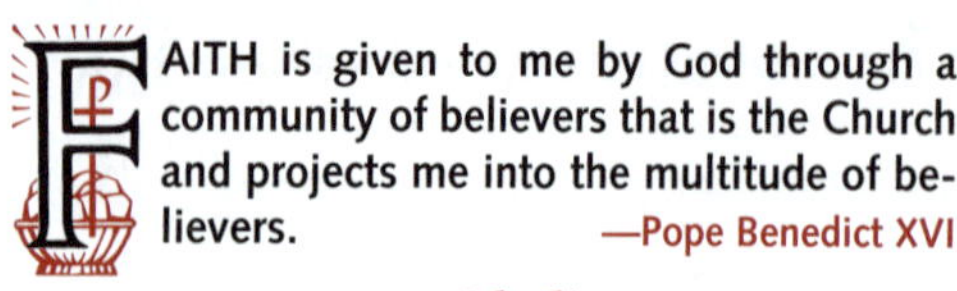

FAITH is given to me by God through a community of believers that is the Church and projects me into the multitude of believers. —Pope Benedict XVI

JAN. 3

I believe...

REFLECTION. By believing, I accept the faith of the whole Church as a rich bequest of truth.

Faith is not my personal opinion. It is an act of trust that what the Church offers as true is true for every age and every person. God gives me the gift of faith through the community of believers; and, by that gift He unites me to Church.

PRAYER. *Lord, keep me one with Your Church.*

FAITH is the daring of the soul to go further than it can see. —William Newton Clarke

JAN. 4

I believe...

REFLECTION. Faith enlarges our understanding beyond what we can see and touch with our physical senses.

By faith, we see all reality as held in existence by God who is outside our empirical experience. We look at the same world unbelievers see and discern a purpose that lifts us up.

PRAYER. *Lord, open my eyes and help me to see all in the light of Your presence.*

Y FAITH, men and women acknowledge fully...the truth of what is revealed because...God himself...is the guarantor of that truth. —Pope St. John Paul II

JAN. 5

I believe...

REFLECTION. To say "I believe" is to accept the truths of the faith that the Church proposes.

Although reason alone cannot arrive at these truths, they are worthy of my intellectual assent because of the witness of Sacred Scripture and Tradition.

PRAYER. *Lord, Your Truth is light to my mind and a path to my feet.*

ELIEVING is an act of the intellect assenting to the divine truth by command of the will moved by God through grace. —St. Thomas Aquinas

JAN. 6

I believe...

REFLECTION. Faith is an act of the intellect by which we accept the truth that God exists. It is also an act of the will by which we entrust ourselves to God.

However, without belief that God exists, we could never respond to Him in obedience and love.

PRAYER. *Lord, lead me by Your grace to know, love, and serve You.*

N ADULT faith does not follow the waves of fashion and the latest novelties. —Pope Benedict XVI

JAN. 7

I believe...

REFLECTION. To believe is a timeless act. It joins me to the vast company of those who in the past have accepted the Gospel handed down from the Apostles.

My faith draws strength from their witness and it breaks the shackles of the present age that would limit me to its own ideology.

PRAYER. *Lord, thank You for keeping me united in the faith of the Apostles.*

AITH is like a bright ray of sun light. It enables us to see God in all things as well as all things in God. —St. Francis de Sales

JAN. 8

I believe...

REFLECTION. Faith gives me a sense of hope. I know that God has a purpose and that He is present, accompanying us in all we do.

My faith inspires me to cooperate with God's grace and will in helping the poor and lonely.

PRAYER. *Lord, help me see Your loving presence in my life.*

MAN is justified by works and not by faith alone. —Jas 2:24

JAN. 9

I believe...

REFLECTION. God Himself initiates a relationship with us through the gift of faith.

The very ability to believe is itself God's gift. And, by this gift of faith, God opens us up to the salvation given in Christ. Sustained by His grace, we attain salvation by living a good life.

PRAYER. *Lord, help me put my faith into action by loving You and my neighbor.*

AITH is to believe what you do not see; the reward of this faith is to see what you believe. —St. Augustine

JAN. 10

I believe...

REFLECTION. We are naturally inquisitive. We constantly ask questions, looking for meaning. Curiosity makes for a happy life, filling us with a sense of adventure and discovery.

The more we know, the greater our self-determination. Faith enlarges our horizon and opens us to knowledge beyond the limit of reason alone.

PRAYER. *Lord, may I seek to know You more.*

THE existence of God is not subjective. He either exists or he doesn't. It's not a matter of opinion. —Ricky Gervais

JAN. 11

I believe in one God...

REFLECTION. We cannot prove God's existence by the empirical sciences. Yet, it makes more sense to truly believe in God who transcends our sensible experience than to embrace the opinion that there is no God.

Without God, the world remains an unexplainable reality, and life a fleeting moment that expires into nothingness.

PRAYER. *O God, You are great and awesome. I give You honor and glory.*

HE WHO trusts in himself is lost. He who trusts in God can do all things. —St. Alphonse Liguori

JAN. 12

I believe in one God...

REFLECTION. My belief in God rescues me from the prison of narcissism. I am not the center of the universe. God is!

My belief in God, therefore, makes me see all of creation and every person as a gift to be treasured and not manipulated for selfish reasons.

PRAYER. *Be exalted, O God, above the heavens let Your glory radiate over all the earth.*

—Ps 57:12

UR heart is restless until it rests in you.
—St. Augustine

JAN. 13

I believe in one God...

REFLECTION. The human spirit is naturally religious. We seek to adore and worship what promises to fulfill our deepest longings.

Because I believe in God, I do not worship the false idols of materialism, success, pleasure or popularity. Only God alone can satisfy the yearnings of my heart.

PRAYER. *My soul longs for you, O God. My soul thirsts for God, the living God.*—Ps 42:2-3

EAR, O Israel, the Lord, our God, is Lord alone. **—Deut 6:4**

JAN. 14

I believe in one God...

REFLECTION. Monotheism is the heart of the Old Testament. As a Christian, I inherit this robust truth of Judaism.

God is the ultimate source of all and reigns supreme over all. This truth impacts my entire life. No state, no ideology, nor any one person can claim my total allegiance. Only God can.

PRAYER. *To You, O God, I offer the homage of my life.*

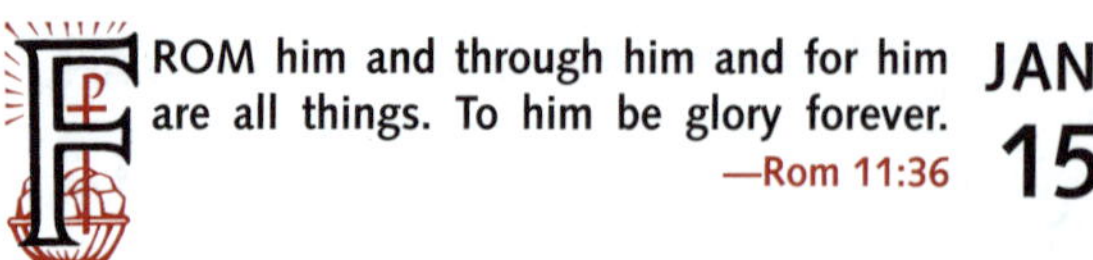

FROM him and through him and for him are all things. To him be glory forever. —Rom 11:36

JAN. 15

I believe in one God...

REFLECTION. From He who is the only God comes all things. From His good bounty, we receive the produce of the land and the very gift of life itself.

Blessed by His generous love, we respond by using His gifts according to His plan with a grateful heart.

PRAYER. *Praise to You, O God, giver of all good gifts. Blessed be Your name.*

THE Lord will guide you continually. —Isa 58:11

JAN. 16

I believe in one God...

REFLECTION. Because of His great love, God who is totally Other bridged the infinite distance separating us from Him.

He gave Moses His name as "I Am Who Am" (Ex 3:14) so that we could know His nearness. As He accompanied Israel in the Exodus, He accompanies each of us, showing us the path that leads us to true happiness.

PRAYER. *O God, lead me in the way of truth.*

E...OFTEN feel weary...yet God brings us through all these things.
—St. Mary MacKillop

JAN. 17

I believe in one God...

REFLECTION. God revealed Himself to Israel as the one true God by breaking the bonds of their slavery.

His ear is ever attentive to the cries of those who suffer oppression. He created us for life and will not abandon us until He can give us the fullness of life.

PRAYER. *In Your compassion, sustain me, O God, with Your strength and wisdom.*

OD cannot change for the better, for He is already perfect; and, being perfect, He cannot change for the worse.
—A.W. Pink

JAN. 18

I believe in one God...

REFLECTION. God's revelation of Himself as the One who is means that He is unchangeable in His essence and attributes.

He is and was and will be forever the same. His very immutability guarantees that He will be forever faithful to His promises.

PRAYER. *Glory to You, O God, for steadfast is Your love.*

[GOD IS] an ineffable mystery before which words...give way to the silence of wonder and worship.

—Pope St. John Paul II

JAN. 19

I believe in one God...

REFLECTION. What we could never know about God by reason, He has made known to us.

In Christ, God has revealed the mystery of His Being as Father, Son and Holy Spirit: one God who exists in the Unity of one substance, yet a Trinity of persons.

PRAYER. *God, mystery beyond all knowing, I adore You.*

THE Father, the Son and the Holy Spirit are one because God is love and love is an absolute life-giving force.

—Pope Benedict XVI

JAN. 20

I believe in one God...

REFLECTION. By sending his only Son and the Holy Spirit, God revealed Himself as an eternal exchange of love: Father, Son and Holy Spirit giving and receiving all that are from each other.

Made in God's image, we become truly human in communion with each other.

PRAYER. *Lord, keep me generous in loving others as You love me.*

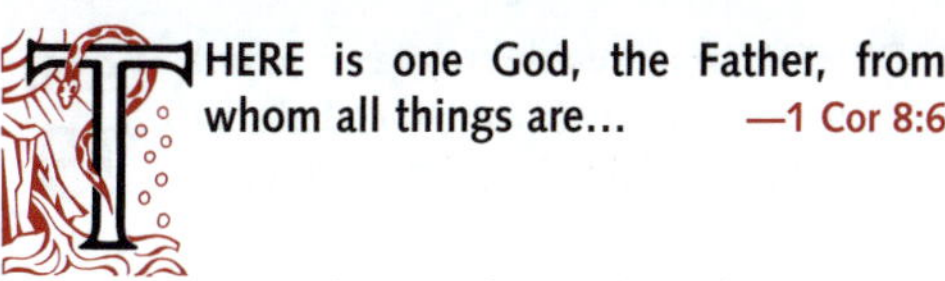

THERE is one God, the Father, from whom all things are... —1 Cor 8:6

JAN. 21

The Father almighty...

REFLECTION. In the *Odyssey*, Homer called Zeus "father of gods and men." But we address God as Father much differently.

No one is His equal. He is the only God, the author of all life. All fatherhood and motherhood come from Him, but He is neither male nor female.

PRAYER. *I praise You, O God, Father of all and source of all life.*

THE same loving Father who cares for you today will care for you tomorrow... —St. Francis de Sales

JAN. 22

The Father almighty...

REFLECTION. God is not an impersonal force. On the first pages of Genesis, God already appears as a Father giving life to Adam and Eve.

As a good Father, He provides for all their needs, keeping them always under His watchful eye. He cares for all of us who are His children.

PRAYER. *O God, I thank You for Your constant care for me.*

HEN Israel was a child, I loved him...out of Egypt, I called my son...I taught Ephraim to walk...
—Hos 11:1, 3

JAN. 23

The Father almighty...

REFLECTION. God chose to enter a special covenant with Israel. He became the Father of the Chosen People, deepening the relationship He already had with them as Creator.

He gave Israel the Law to teach all of us how to live as His children.

PRAYER. *Father, guide my steps in the path of justice and truth.*

HE Father has chosen to give you the kingdom.
—Lk 12:32

JAN. 24

The Father almighty...

REFLECTION. The Old Testament rarely images God as Father. But "Father" is Jesus' favorite way of speaking about God.

Sixty-five times in the gospels of Matthew, Mark and Luke and one hundred times in John, He speaks of God as Father. Jesus would have us confidently approach God, ever eager to lavish on us the wealth of His kingdom.

PRAYER. *Father, I trust Your great goodness to me knowing the love You have for Your Son.*

HE whole mystery of Christian prayer is summed up in this one word: Father.
—Pope Francis

JAN. 25

The Father almighty...

REFLECTION. In His prayer, Jesus addressed God as "*Abba*." This Aramaic word children use to address their father conveys both their affection and trust for their father who loves them.

With His use of the word "*Abba*," Jesus thus teaches us the shocking accessibility of God.

PRAYER. *I praise You, Abba, Father. You are ever near and attentive to me.*

RYING to build the brotherhood of man without the fatherhood of God is like trying to make a wheel without a hub.
—Irene Dunne

JAN. 26

The Father almighty...

REFLECTION. In giving us the *Our Father*, Jesus revealed the secret to build the human community. To address God as *our* Father is to acknowledge that we are one with all others.

We all depend on God's goodness. We pray for *our* daily bread and for forgiveness of *our* trespasses.

PRAYER. *Father, unite us in Your expansive love.*

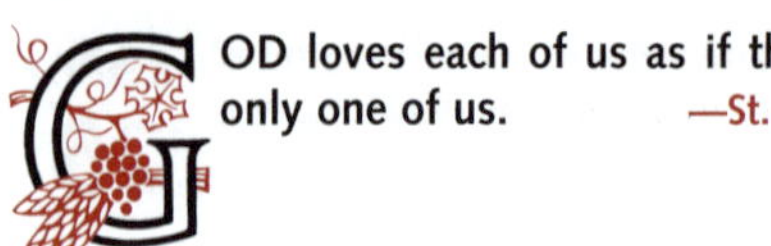

OD loves each of us as if there were only one of us. —St. Augustine

JAN. 27

The Father almighty...

REFLECTION. In the parable of the Prodigal Son, Jesus exemplifies God the Father's unfathomable love for all His children.

Both the rebellious younger son and the unforgiving elder son offend the father. Yet, he opens his arms to welcome both to share the joy of being his family.

PRAYER. *Your kindness, [O God], is a greater joy than life itself.*—Ps 63:4

OD sent his Son, born of a woman,... so that we might receive adoption as sons. —Gal 4:4-5

JAN. 28

The Father almighty...

REFLECTION. Jesus' relationship to the Father is not the same as ours. He tells Mary Magdalene on Easter morning, "I am ascending to my Father and your Father, to my God and your God" (Jn 20:17).

Jesus is the Eternal Son of the Father. We share in His Sonship by grace.

PRAYER. *I praise You, Father, for making me Yours in Christ.*

THE whole Christian life is a communion with each of the Divine Persons... Everyone who glorifies the Father does so through the Son in the Holy Spirit.

—*Catechism of the Catholic Church*, 259

JAN. 29

The Father almighty...

REFLECTION. In revealing His unique relationship to the Father, Jesus revealed God as Father and Son in an eternal, reciprocal relationship.

He also revealed their eternal relationship to the Holy Spirit. Jesus invites us to live this great mystery.

PRAYER. *All glory to You, O Blessed Trinity!*

NOTHING will be impossible for God.

—Lk 1:37

JAN. 30

The Father almighty...

REFLECTION. The English word "almighty" translates the Greek word "*pantokrator*" (literally, all-sovereign) in the Creed. This word denotes omnipotence. In Sacred Scripture, it expresses the fact that God rules over history and creation.

All things are subject to His power. God can do anything He wills. Because God is almighty, we can confidently turn to Him in all our needs.

PRAYER. *With Your great power, guide and defend us, O God.*

GOD makes all things work together for those who love him. —Rom 8:28

JAN. 31

The Father almighty...

REFLECTION. The unimaginable power of God both inspires us with awe and causes us to wonder. Since God can do all things, why does He not prevent bad things from happening?

As Isaiah reminds us, God's thoughts are far beyond our thoughts (Isa 55:9). In ways that we cannot fathom, God uses His power for our ultimate good.

PRAYER. *Father, help me to trust Your all-powerful wisdom especially when bad things happen.*

O LORD...in your hands are power and might, and there is no one who can withstand you. —2 Chr 20:6

FEB. 1

The Father almighty...

REFLECTION. In raising up a son for the aged Abraham, God showed His power over creation. This faintly foreshadowed His omnipotence in raising up His beloved Son Jesus from the dead.

The all-powerful God is always at work to bring us to the fullness of life.

PRAYER. *Your great power, O Lord, is my strength and my life.*

RUST the past to God's mercy, the present to God's love and the future to God's providence. —St. Augustine

FEB. 2

The Father almighty...

REFLECTION. Scripture mentions God's providence for the first time when God provides a ram for Abraham to sacrifice instead of his son Isaac.

Abraham names that place *Yahweh-yireh* (literally, "the Lord will provide"—Gen 22:14). God's providence embraces every aspect of our lives even to the number of hairs on our head (Mt 10:30).

PRAYER. *In You, O God, I place my life.*

AVE confidence in prayer. It is the unfailing power which God has given us.
—St. Peter Julian Eymard

FEB. 3

The Father almighty...

REFLECTION. In the first hymn recorded in the Acts of the Apostles, the first Christians praised God as *Despotes* (Acts 4:24-30).

This Greek word, used only three times in the New Testament, addresses God as the absolute Master of the Universe. God's almighty power grounds our confidence to pray to Him at all times.

PRAYER. *Increase, O God, my confidence in You and Your power.*

HE beginning of the world...derives directly from a Supreme Origin that creates out of love. —Pope Francis

FEB. 4

...maker of heaven and earth...

REFLECTION. With these words, the Creed sums up the very first words of Scripture: "In the beginning, God created the heavens and the earth" (Gen 1:1).

Creation is not a one-time act in the distant past. God is continually bringing all that is into existence and sustaining it by His power.

PRAYER. *I thank You, O God, for giving life to all things.*

IME is short. Eternity is long.... This short life [should] be lived in the light of eternity. —Charles Spurgeon

FEB. 5

...maker of heaven and earth...

REFLECTION. Creation had a beginning. From His fingertips, God let fall a tiny point of energy that expanded into all that exists.

Time and space and matter came to be at His command. God Himself is outside of creation.

PRAYER. *God, help me use my time well in this world so that I may spend eternity with You.*

EFORE the mountains were brought forth or earth and the world came into existence, from everlasting to everlasting you are God. —Ps 90:2

FEB. 6

...maker of heaven and earth...

REFLECTION. From all eternity, before there was time, God exists. He is above and outside the world He has created.

But, He is ever near and close to His creatures. The physical laws of the universe are but His servants.

PRAYER. *How awesome Your power, O God, that rules all of creation.*

CIENCE and religion are not antagonists. On the contrary, they are sisters. —Wernher von Braun

FEB. 7

...maker of heaven and earth...

REFLECTION. Many say that science and faith are incompatible. But it was belief in a God who created a world with order that gave birth to science which seeks to discover that order.

Francis Bacon, the first to develop a scientific method, was a devout Christian.

PRAYER. *You have ordered all things wisely, O Creator God.*

LORD, You have made us for yourself, and our hearts are restless until they rest in you. —St. Augustine

FEB. 8

...maker of heaven and earth...

REFLECTION. Science can tell how the world is made, but not why it was made. Scripture, however, reveals that God created the world to share His own divine life with us.

By using the things of this world according to God's will, we come to enjoy the God of all things.

PRAYER. *Grant me Your grace, O God, to use Your gifts wisely.*

HERE are not laws without a lawgiver. —Albert Einstein

FEB. 9

...maker of heaven and earth...

REFLECTION. The universe is governed by laws of physics and chemistry. The slightest change in these fundamental forces at work in the universe would make life on the earth unsustainable.

Yet, there is order and life. Reason whispers to us that a wise lawgiver guides creation for our good. And this lawgiver is God.

PRAYER. *In Your goodness, O God, You give us life and peace.*

OD to me is a mystery, but is the explanation for the miracle of existence.
—Allan Sandage

FEB. 10

...maker of heaven and earth...

REFLECTION. God who creates all things gives life to every living creature.

Science can dissect and discover the secrets of life itself, but no scientific experiment can create life from nothing or from something that is not already alive. God's very existence grounds the possibility and the fact of all life.

PRAYER. *Renew, O God, Your life within me, so that I may give You glory.*

IRACLES are not in contradiction to nature. They are only in contradiction with what we know of nature.
—St. Augustine

FEB. 11

...maker of heaven and earth...

REFLECTION. God allows the laws of nature to work their predictable results.

In every miracle, however, He accomplishes to our wonderment what nature cannot do on her own. He momentarily draws back the veil to make us see that He truly is in control.

PRAYER. *To You, God of power and might, be praise and glory.*

OD reveals himself in the orderly harmony of what exists. —Albert Einstein

FEB. 12

...maker of heaven and earth...

REFLECTION. The incredible harmony of the universe left Isaac Newton, a key figure in the 17th century Scientific Revolution, in awe.

His scientific observations of the arrangement and movement of the sun, the planets, and the vast array of heavenly bodies led him to acknowledge "the counsel and dominion of an intelligent and powerful Being."

PRAYER. *All Your works, O God, proclaim Your glory and love.*

HAT the eye with all its inimitable contrivances... could have been formed by natural selection seems...absurd in the highest degree. —Charles Darwin

FEB. 13

...maker of heaven and earth...

REFLECTION. Werner Arber, the 1978 Nobel Prize winner in Medicine and Physiology, said that he could not explain how several hundred different specific macro-molecules form the most primitive cells.

To say this just happens requires a faith greater than the reasonable belief in God as Creator.

PRAYER. *Creation unfolds, O God, the beauty of Your wisdom.*

RTISTIC expressions are…highways to God, the supreme Beauty.

—Pope Benedict XVI

FEB. 14

…maker of heaven and earth…

REFLECTION. Michelangelo's Sistine Chapel frescoes leave us in awe. Handel's *Hallelujah Chorus* lifts us to our feet in joy.

All beauty springs from the genius and intelligence of the artist and indirectly point to God who wishes us to find joy and pleasure in this world as a foretaste of heaven.

PRAYER. *O God, draw me to Yourself, the source of all beauty.*

EFORE the foundation of the world, he chose us in Christ to be holy and blameless…and filled with love. —Eph 1:4

FEB. 15

…maker of heaven and earth…

REFLECTION. Neither chance nor necessity brought the universe into existence. All exists for a purpose. God freely created us.

Made in His image, He gifts us with freedom so that we could enter into a personal relationship with Him. Choosing what God wills makes us truly free.

PRAYER. *Enlighten my will, O God, to love You above all things.*

VERYTHING created by God is good… —1 Tim 4:4

FEB. 16

…of all things visible and invisible…

REFLECTION. In the 2nd century, Marcion taught that the evil God of the Old Testament created the visible, material universe which is evil and that the God of Jesus created the unseen spiritual world which is good.

Against this Gnostic dualism, we hold that the one God created everything, material and spiritual, as good.

PRAYER. *O God, from Your hands, we receive all that is good.*

AKE care of your body as if you were going to live forever; and take care of your soul as if you were going to die tomorrow. —St. Augustine

FEB. 17

…of all things visible and invisible…

REFLECTION. Many limited their understanding to "things" that they experience with their senses. But there is more to creation than meets the eye.

God who has created our physical body creates in each of us a spiritual, immortal soul.

PRAYER. *How wonderfully You have made me, O Lord.*

GOD formed man out of the dust of the earth...and breathed his breath of life into his nostrils... —Gen 2:7

FEB. 18

...of all things visible and invisible...

REFLECTION. Created in God's image, we are both material and spiritual. From our parents, we receive our body.

However, directly from God, we receive our soul. When our body dies, our soul (our thinking, loving self) continues to live. We do not perish. We are destined for eternal life.

PRAYER. *Lord, You endow me with great dignity as a child of God.*

WE HAVE an immortal soul, that we may use every means to prepare ourselves for that other life. —St. John Chrysostom

FEB. 19

...of all things visible and invisible...

REFLECTION. The deacon Stephen was the first Christian martyr.

As his body was being pummeled to death with rocks, he fell to the ground, asking Jesus to receive his spirit (Acts 7:59). He knew that his soul would continue to live in God's Presence.

PRAYER. *Lord, help me see beyond the things of this world.*

EVERY visible thing in this world is put in the charge of an angel. —St. Augustine

FEB. 20

...of all things visible and invisible...

REFLECTION. Unlike people of antiquity, many in our post-modern world dismiss the existence of angels and demons. Yet Scripture mentions angels 273 times.

And the New Testament speaks of fallen angels or demons at least 80 times. God created the angels as pure spirits to cooperate with Him in His plan for all creation.

PRAYER. *God, we thank You for angels who protect us from demons.*

OFTEN God intervenes on our behalf through the use of His angels. —Billy Graham

FEB. 21

...of all things visible and invisible...

REFLECTION. Angels are pure spirits. They have no body. Sometimes they appeared by taking a human form.

Abraham at Mamre, Gideon, the women at Jesus' tomb, the apostles at the Ascension, and Peter in prison are among those who saw angels sent in human form to help them. Angels act at God's command for our welfare.

PRAYER. *You care for me, O gracious God, beyond reckoning.*

GOD is the brightest of lights which can never be extinguished, and the choirs of angels radiate [His] light.

—St. Hildegard of Bingen

FEB. 22

...of all things visible and invisible...

REFLECTION. The number of angels is too great to count "myriads, thousands upon thousands..." (Ps 68:18).

St. Gregory the Great classified angelic beings as Seraphim, Cherubim, and Thrones who contemplate God; Dominions, Virtues, and Powers who govern the universe; and, Principalities, Archangels, and Angels sent as God's messengers.

PRAYER. *Your light, O God, fills heaven and earth.*

ANGELS are both God's messengers and God's message, witness to eternity in time,...the divine amidst the ordinary.

—Forrest Church

FEB. 23

...of all things visible and invisible...

REFLECTION. The word "angel" from the Greek means messenger. Angels warned Abraham and Lot to flee Sodom and Gomorrah.

Gabriel announced John the Baptist's birth to Zechariah and Jesus' birth to Mary. To shepherds, they announced His coming; and, to the women at the tomb, His Resurrection.

PRAYER. *Lord, may Your holy angels inspire me to do Your will.*

RE not all angels ministering spirits sent forth to serve...those who will inherit salvation? —Heb 1:14

FEB. 24

...of all things visible and invisible...

REFLECTION. Angels advance God's plan for His people. An angel called Gideon to form an army (Jdg 6).

An angel strengthened the despondent Elijah to continue His prophetic mission (1 Ki 19). An angel guaranteed the safety of Paul after a shipwreck on his way to Rome (Acts 27:23-24).

PRAYER. *Lord, send forth Your angels to help me follow Your will.*

WILL send an angel before you...to bring you to the place which I have prepared. —Ex 23:20

FEB. 25

...of all things visible and invisible...

REFLECTION. In 1916, an angel appeared to Lucia dos Santos, Francisco and Jacinta Marto preparing them for the apparition of Our Lady of Fatima in 1917.

He identified himself as the Angel of Portugal. An angel guided Israel during the Exodus; and, according to Daniel 10:13-21, an angel guides every nation.

PRAYER. *Lord, guide all nations with Your angels to bring peace on earth.*

NGELS, who, though invisible, are always with you. —St. Francis de Sales

FEB. 26

...of all things visible and invisible...

REFLECTION. When Pharaoh obstinately refused to let the Hebrew slaves leave Egypt, an angel struck down every firstborn son (Ex 12:12-23).

At night an angel struck down Sennacherib's army poised to destroy Jerusalem. At the end of time, angels will execute God's judgment on the world (Rev 7:1; 8-10).

PRAYER. *Thank You Lord, for surrounding me with Your holy angels.*

ESIDE each believer stands an angel as protector and shepherd, leading him to life. —St. Basil

FEB. 27

...of all things visible and invisible...

REFLECTION. So great is God's love that, from the moment of our conception until death, He surrounds us with the protection and intercession of a guardian angel.

Jesus once said that our guardian angels who watch over us constantly gaze on God's face while caring for us (Mt 18:10).

PRAYER. *Angel of God, my guardian, ever be at my side.*

HE finest trick of the devil is to persuade you that he does not exist.

—Charles Baudelaire

FEB. 28

...of all things visible and invisible...

REFLECTION. After creating countless angels, God put them to the test before admitting them to heaven. With pride, some refused to accept God's will for them and creation.

As pure spiritual creatures, their sin of rebellion was irrevocable. They doomed themselves to eternal punishment. Chief among these fallen angels or demons is Satan.

PRAYER. *Preserve me, Lord, from all evil now and at the hour of my death.*

E ARE not struggling against flesh and blood, but against...the spirits of evil.

—Eph 6:12

FEB. 29

...of all things visible and invisible...

REFLECTION. Envious of God's plan to share His very life with us in Christ, Satan tried to turn Jesus from His mission for our salvation.

God allows Satan and his devils to tempt us, not to make us sin, but to strengthen us in our resolve to love and serve God above all.

PRAYER. *Grant me, O Lord, the grace to avoid sin and the temptation to sin.*

AINT Michael is the sword in God's right hand.
—Joyce Kilmer

MAR. 1

...of all things visible and invisible...

REFLECTION. When a 6th century plague ravaged Rome, St. Michael the Archangel appeared to Pope St. Gregory the Great sheathing his sword and ending the plague.

Michael, named four times in the Scriptures, cast Satan and his minions from heaven. He is prince of the heavenly hosts, guardian of the Church, and our protector in the battle with evil.

PRAYER. *St. Michael, defend us in battle.*

[

HRIST]...is at the right hand of God, with angels and authorities and powers, made subject to Him.
—1 Pet 3:22

MAR. 2

...of all things visible and invisible...

REFLECTION. The angels are subject to the Risen Lord Jesus. Since they were "created through him and for him" (Col 1:16), we honor but do not adore them.

At the end of time, Christ will send out His angels to separate the righteous from the evil (Mt 13:49).

PRAYER. *May Your holy angels lead me to Paradise with You.*

MAR. 3

IS THERE a greater happiness than to imitate on earth the choir of angels?

—St. Basil the Great

...of all things visible and invisible...

REFLECTION. The prophet Isaiah saw angels worshiping at God's throne (Isa 6:3). Likewise, in his vision of heaven, the author of Revelation saw them worshiping God (Rev 5:11).

At Jesus' birth, angels filled the heavens with praise. The psalmist often calls on the angels to worship God (Ps 103:20; Ps 148:2).

PRAYER. *With the angels, Lord, I praise You and give You glory.*

MAR. 4

HEN Mass is being celebrated, the sanctuary is filled with countless angels who adore the Divine Victim immolated on the altar.

—St. John Chrysostom

...of all things visible and invisible...

REFLECTION. In every liturgy, angels join us in worship.

They carry our prayers up to God like incense; and, we unite our praise of God with theirs, crying out, "Holy, Holy, Holy, Lord God of hosts." Every church is God's earthly dwelling place.

PRAYER. *Holy Lord, I worship You whom all angels adore and glorify.*

FAITH is the strength by which a shattered world shall emerge into the light.

—Helen Keller

MAR. 5

...of all things visible and invisible...

REFLECTION. With the eyes of our body, we behold the world in all its wonder.

But with the gift of faith, we crack open the shell of mundane reality and see the presence of God who orders all things for our good. Faith enables us to see reality as it truly is.

PRAYER. *Lord, increase my faith to see You in all things even as my vision may fail.*

SPEAK but the name of Jesus, the clouds disperse, and peace descends anew from heaven.

—St. Bernard

MAR. 6

...I believe in one Lord Jesus Christ...

REFLECTION. The angel Gabriel gave Jesus His name before His birth, a name that means "God saves."

In Jesus of Nazareth, God brings to fulfillment His plan of salvation for the whole world. "Everyone who calls on the name of the Lord will be saved" (Rom 10:13).

PRAYER. *Lord Jesus, deliver me and save me from my sins.*

BEING Christian is not the result of...a lofty idea, but the encounter with an event, a person, which gives life a new horizon... —Pope Benedict XVI

MAR. 7

...I believe in one Lord Jesus Christ...

REFLECTION. We commit our lives not to a philosophy of life but to the person of Jesus who walked this earth.

Our faith is grounded firmly in what God has done in Jesus. Jesus is the center of our lives. Faith opens our eyes to Jesus' presence in every event of our lives and enables us to develop an intimate friendship with Him.

PRAYER. *To You, O Jesus, I give myself.*

JESUS is not one of many ways to approach God, nor is He the best of several ways; He is the only way. —A. W. Tozer

MAR. 8

...I believe in one Lord Jesus Christ...

REFLECTION. We accept Jesus not simply as a teacher of truth like Confucius or a prophet like Elijah. No!

He is the one Savior of the entire world. Only in Him is the fullness of truth and the gift of eternal life.

PRAYER. *You alone, O Jesus, are my hope.*

THE End came forward into the present in Jesus the Messiah. —N. T. Wright

MAR. 9

...I believe in one Lord Jesus Christ...

REFLECTION. The title "Christ" means "the Anointed One" (in Hebrew, "Messiah").

The Father anointed Jesus with the Holy Spirit at His baptism not to establish a political kingdom for one nation but to usher in the end time when all people could enter the Kingdom of God.

PRAYER. *Christ Jesus, help me live today as belonging to God's Kingdom.*

A CHRISTIAN does not announce himself, he announces another, prepares the way for another: the Lord.

—Pope Francis

MAR. 10

...I believe in one Lord Jesus Christ...

REFLECTION. When the religious leaders of the Jews questioned John the Baptist about his ministry, he pointed directly to Jesus.

John's baptism with water was a preparation for Jesus who would baptize with the Holy Spirit (Mt 3:11). Jesus, not John, was the long-awaited Messiah.

PRAYER. *Christ Jesus, help me to lead others to You as John the Baptist did.*

OVE is shown more in deeds than in words. —St. Ignatius of Loyola

MAR. 11

...I believe in one Lord Jesus Christ...

REFLECTION. Once John the Baptist recognized Jesus as the Messiah, he directed his disciples to follow Him (Jn 1:35-51).

What humility! What unselfishness! John sought no acclaim for himself, but what was good for others. This is the meaning of love. It is doing what is good for others.

PRAYER. *Christ Jesus, help me imitate the humble love of John the Baptist.*

O BE a disciple is to be committed to...following Him every day. —Billy Graham

MAR. 12

...I believe in one Lord Jesus Christ...

REFLECTION. Pointing Jesus out as the Messiah, the Baptist sang the swan song of Old Testament prophecy.

Andrew and another of John's disciples immediately follow Jesus and Jesus speaks His first words as Messiah, inviting them to stay with Him. (Jn 1:39). This is the essence of all Christian discipleship: being with Jesus.

PRAYER. *Jesus, help me stay with You always.*

EPENTANCE is a gift of God's grace.
—R. Tagore

MAR. 13

...I believe in one Lord Jesus Christ...

REFLECTION. When John the Baptist was arrested, his voice fell silent, but not his message. Jesus began preaching in Galilee, issuing the same summons to repentance, but with a difference. Jesus proclaims, "The time of fulfillment has arrived...Repent..." (Mk 1:15).

In Jesus, God is now fulfilling His promise of saving us, enabling us to turn from sin.

PRAYER. *Lord, grant me the grace of true repentance.*

ISCIPLESHIP isn't a program...it's a way of life. It's not for a limited time, but for our whole life. **—Bill Hull**

MAR. 14

...I believe in one Lord Jesus Christ...

REFLECTION. Beginning His Galilean ministry, Jesus gathers around Himself others willing to follow Him, ushering in God's kingdom on earth. Jesus calls His first four disciples, Peter and Andrew, James and John.

Recognizing Him as sent by God, they leave behind their former lives to become His disciples.

PRAYER. *Jesus, help me follow You today and forever.*

HE human soul is the battlefield between God and Satan. —Padre Pio

MAR. 15

...I believe in one Lord Jesus Christ...

REFLECTION. At His first public miracle in Capernaum, Jesus casts out a demon from a possessed man in the synagogue (Mk 1:23-26).

Throughout His entire ministry, Jesus confronts the Evil One. The real battle on the world's stage is between good and evil. At Jesus' word, demons flee. No power can resist His divine command.

PRAYER. *Jesus, drive from me all evil and strengthen me to always resist it.*

HRIST is at work for you in heaven; he makes intercession for you. —Thomas Watson

MAR. 16

...I believe in one Lord Jesus Christ...

REFLECTION. At the Last Supper, Jesus warned His apostles that Satan wished to sift all of [them] like wheat (Lk 22:31–32).

But they had no need to "fear the one who can destroy both soul and body in Gehenna" (Mt 10:28), because Jesus Himself would be praying to the Father for His followers.

PRAYER. *Jesus, pray for me!*

HERE are two views which the Christian ought to cultivate...the Devil's back and the face of God. —Kent Hughes

MAR. 17

...I believe in one Lord Jesus Christ...

REFLECTION. Jesus gave the Twelve Apostles and other disciples the authority to cast out demons (Mt 10:1; Lk 10:17).

He equips all His disciples with the power to destroy Satan's grip on the world. By avoiding sin and living in union with Jesus, we rid the world of Satan's power.

PRAYER. *Father, help me to pray "deliver us from evil" with conviction.*

HE Savior is glad to save, and the sinner is glad to be saved.

—Charles Spurgeon

MAR. 18

...I believe in one Lord Jesus Christ...

REFLECTION. The disciples had success in releasing others from bondage to Satan.

All the while, Jesus was watching and praying as He saw "Satan fall from heaven like lightning" (Lk 10:18). His heart was filled with joy as sinners returned to God's grace. Where Satan is defeated, joy abounds.

PRAYER. *Jesus, may Your victory over sin bring me great joy.*

JESUS has given you the power to live as He lived, which is something no earthly teacher can do. —James Robison

MAR. 19

...I believe in one Lord Jesus Christ...

REFLECTION. In the gospels, Jesus is most often called "teacher" (forty-five times) or, in Hebrew, "rabbi" (twelve times).

And rightly so! Amid the droll succession of teachers the world has known, Jesus is the most inspiring. For us, His words are truly "spirit and life" (Jn 6:63).

PRAYER. *Teach me, Jesus, to know, love, and serve Your Father like You.*

THEY were not to proclaim an idea, but to witness to a person. —Pope Benedict XVI

MAR. 20

...I believe in one Lord Jesus Christ...

REFLECTION. Unlike Jewish students who chose to study under a particular rabbi, Jesus chose His disciples to be with Him.

Whereas the Torah was central for Jewish disciples of a rabbi, for the disciples of Jesus, He was the truth that they longed to know and imitate.

PRAYER. *Jesus, open my heart to know You who are Truth itself.*

OD made [you]...He knows how to recreate what He created...

—St. Augustine

MAR. 21

...I believe in one Lord Jesus Christ...

REFLECTION. The gospels record twenty-six individual healings and mention many others (Mt 4:23-25) that Jesus did during His short public ministry.

As Jesus told John the Baptist, His healings were signs that He indeed was the Messiah (Lk 7:20-23). He makes visible God's will that we be whole in mind, body, and spirit.

PRAYER. *Jesus, Divine Physician, heal me, body and soul.*

HE greatest healing therapy is friendship and love. —Hubert H. Humphrey

MAR. 22

...I believe in one Lord Jesus Christ...

REFLECTION. Jesus, the Divine Physician, lived our human condition as we do with its pain, suffering, and even death itself.

Loving others, He healed many and sent His disciples to cure the sick (Mt 10:8; Lk 9:2; 10:9). His work of healing continues in our care for the sick and wounded among us.

PRAYER. *Jesus, make me truly love the sick and suffering.*

JESUS is greater than our enemy. He can... deliver us from anything the enemy takes from us. —Mistie House

MAR. 23

...I believe in one Lord Jesus Christ...

REFLECTION. The Jews acclaimed every Davidic king as a son of God.

When they called Jesus the Son of God, therefore, they were expressing their belief that Jesus, as the anointed heir to David's throne, was going to free them from the oppressive tyranny of Rome in their day.

PRAYER. *Jesus, deliver me from every evil.*

THE only significance of life consists in helping to establish the kingdom of God. —Leo Tolstoy

MAR. 24

...I believe in one Lord Jesus Christ...

REFLECTION. As the Son of David, the long-awaited Messiah, Jesus came not to restore one nation to its former glory but to usher all peoples into the kingdom of God.

He was not a political leader like any of Israel's kings. As Messiah, He established God's kingdom forever (Mk 12:35-37).

PRAYER. *Son of David, keep me and my family safe in God's kingdom.*

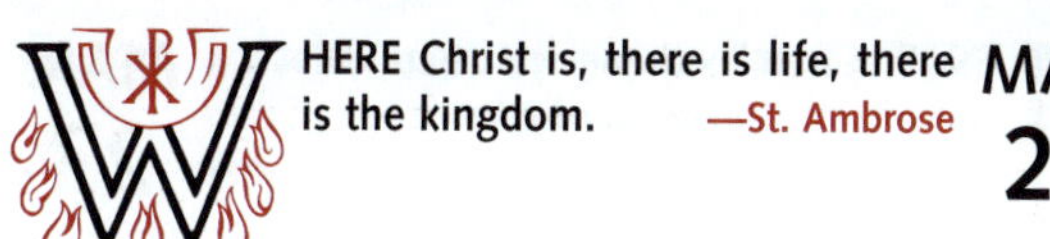

HERE Christ is, there is life, there is the kingdom. —St. Ambrose

MAR. 25

...I believe in one Lord Jesus Christ...

REFLECTION. God promised David that He would establish his throne forever (2 Sam 7:12-16).

David's kingdom came to end; but, God remained faithful to His promise. In a way beyond all expectation, in Jesus, God fulfilled His promise. When we accept Jesus as our Savior, we enter His kingdom that will last forever.

PRAYER. *Jesus, Son of David, I believe that in You is eternal life.*

PART from the cross there is no other ladder by which we may get to heaven. —St. Rose of Lima

MAR. 26

...I believe in one Lord Jesus Christ...

REFLECTION. When Jesus left Jericho in the last week of His life, the blind beggar Bartimaeus cried out, "Jesus, Son of David, have pity on me" (Mk 10:45-52).

Once Jesus healed him, Bartimaeus, with eyes wide open, followed Jesus on the way to the Cross.

PRAYER. *Jesus, like Bartimaeus keep me on the path of true discipleship.*

ESUS set an example for us to follow: a life of loving, obedient service.

—Charles F. Stanley

MAR. 27

...I believe in one Lord Jesus Christ...

REFLECTION. When the pagan centurion at the Cross recognized Jesus' moral goodness, he called Him "a son of God" (Mt 27:54).

Jesus was such a virtuous and righteous individual that even those without faith could see His goodness. He embodied all that is good about our human nature.

PRAYER. *Jesus, help me follow Your good example in all things.*

E WAS...Son of God in the spirit and Son of man in the flesh, that is, both God and man.

—Lactantius

MAR. 28

...I believe in one Lord Jesus Christ...

REFLECTION. Jesus referred to Himself most often as the Son of Man.

This title from Daniel 7:13–14 speaks of a divine figure from heaven with authority and sovereign power. Because Jesus is the Son of Man, He can forgive sins and cure disease (Lk 5:23).

PRAYER. *Jesus, thank You for making me whole in body and spirit.*

HE Kingdom of God is a kingdom of paradox.... Victory comes through defeat.
—Charles Colson

MAR. 29

...I believe in one Lord Jesus Christ...

REFLECTION. When Jesus speaks about the Son of Man, he often does so with reference to His suffering and death (Mk 10:45).

By joining His human suffering and death with His divine role as Son of Man, Jesus teaches us that His Cross ushers in the definitive inauguration of God's kingdom.

PRAYER. *Jesus, keep me united with You even in suffering.*

RUTH stands for time and eternity.
—Billy Graham

MAR. 30

...I believe in one Lord Jesus Christ...

REFLECTION. Questioned by the high priest about His identity, Jesus proclaims the truth.

He is not only the Messiah but the Son of Man who shares in the very divinity of God (Mk 14:61-62). Jesus is more than a teacher, greater than a prophet, more powerful than a miracle worker. He is truly divine.

PRAYER. *Jesus, keep me ever aware of who You are: the One true God.*

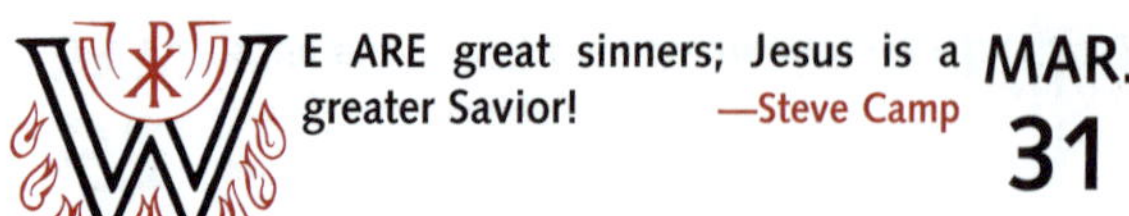

WE ARE great sinners; Jesus is a greater Savior! —Steve Camp

MAR. 31

...I believe in one Lord Jesus Christ...

REFLECTION. During His public ministry, Jesus spent two days with the people of Samaria (Jn 4:40). The many who came to believe in Him gave Him the same title given to Roman emperors from Caesar to Hadrian.

They called Him "the Savior of the world" (Jn 4:42). Jesus transcends all national boundaries. He comes for all peoples.

PRAYER. *Savior of the world, thank You for saving all of us!*

THIS bread satisfies the inner longings and hungers of the human heart.

—Billy Graham

APR. 1

...I believe in one Lord Jesus Christ...

REFLECTION. In the synagogue of Capernaum, Jesus said, "I am the bread of life" (Jn 6:48).

As bread, the most basic of foods nourishes the body, Jesus nourishes our minds with truth and our hearts with love. To truly live now and forever, we must nourish ourselves on His every word.

PRAYER. *Jesus, be the source of all the good that I do.*

INCE Christ Himself has said, "This is My Body," who shall dare to doubt that it is His Body? —St. Cyril of Jerusalem

APR. 2

...I believe in one Lord Jesus Christ...

REFLECTION. At the Last Supper, Jesus fulfilled what He promised in Capernaum. He gave us the Eucharist as the Bread of Life.

The Eucharist is truly Jesus, Body, Blood, Soul, and Divinity, who comes to dwell with us, making us one with Him.

PRAYER. *Jesus, I worship You truly as the Bread of Life and long to receive You.*

SACRAMENT of devotion! O sign of unity! O bond of charity! —St. Augustine

APR. 3

...I believe in one Lord Jesus Christ...

REFLECTION. St. Paul teaches that we who eat the one Bread of Life become the one body of Christ (1 Cor 10:17).

The Eucharist draws us close to Jesus and into deeper communion with each other. The Eucharist impels us to love all those who share this great mystery of God's love.

PRAYER. *Jesus, Bread of Life, keep us united in love of You and the Eucharist.*

THE one bread...provides the medicine of immortality, the antidote for death, and the food that makes us live forever... —St. Ignatius of Antioch

APR. 4

...I believe in one Lord Jesus Christ...

REFLECTION. In receiving the Eucharist, we receive Jesus who draws us more deeply into His work of redemption.

He floods our soul with His grace, giving us the pledge of the life to come. Already we anticipate the glory of heaven.

PRAYER. *Jesus, Bread of Life, bring me to the glory of heaven.*

CHRIST is the eternal splendor enlightening our minds and hearts. —St. Ambrose

APR. 5

...I believe in one Lord Jesus Christ...

REFLECTION. When the Feast of Tabernacles ended, the seventy-five foot high Temple lamps were lit.

With Jerusalem itself ablaze with their light, Jesus proclaimed, "I am the light of the world" (Jn 8:12). Not for one city or nation, but for the entire world, Jesus brings God's truth, dispelling the darkness of error.

PRAYER. *Jesus, fill me with the light of Your truth and wisdom.*

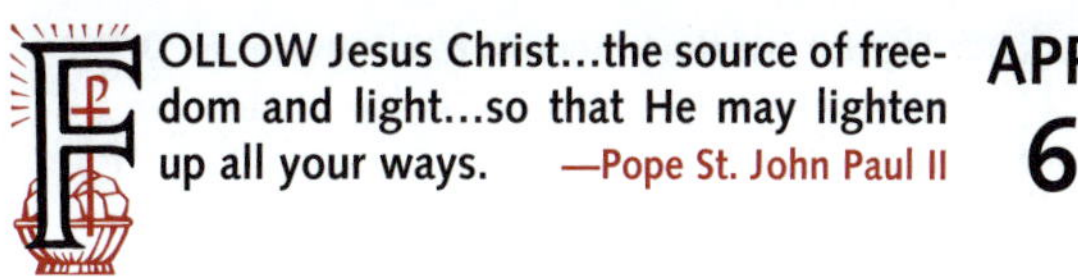

FOLLOW Jesus Christ...the source of freedom and light...so that He may lighten up all your ways. —Pope St. John Paul II

APR. 6

...I believe in one Lord Jesus Christ...

REFLECTION. During their wilderness wanderings, God guided His people at night with the pillar of fire.

Following it, the Israelites found safe passage on the way to the Promised Land. Following Jesus, the Light of the world, is the sure way to heaven's glory.

PRAYER. *Jesus, be my guide every step of the way so that I will follow where You lead me.*

HE IS...the only Lord on whom we should depend...

—St. Louis Marie de Montfort

APR. 7

...I believe in one Lord Jesus Christ...

REFLECTION. In the sheepfold, the sheep find safety from all danger. Speaking of Himself as the Good Shepherd and the sheepfold, Jesus said "I am the gate" (Jn 10:9).

Jesus provides us with safety from all dangers, from every peril that would destroy us. He secures for us the blessing of peace and eternal life.

PRAYER. *Jesus, my shepherd, in You is my safety and salvation.*

HE duty of the branch is to cling to the vine. —Max Lucado

APR. 8

...I believe in one Lord Jesus Christ...

REFLECTION. At the Last Supper, Jesus said, "I am the vine, you are the branches" (Jn 15:5).

United to Christ, He fills us with the Holy Spirit so that, with the same love that He has for us, we might bear the rich fruit of charity and self-sacrifice in the world.

PRAYER. *Holy Spirit, fill me and move me to do acts of mercy.*

HE vinedresser is never nearer the branches than when he is pruning them. —David Jeremiah

APR. 9

...I believe in one Lord Jesus Christ...

REFLECTION. Jesus is the true vine; and, the Father who is the vinedresser prunes away every dead branch bearing disease and decay (Jn 15:1-2).

He works to remove from us all those vices and imperfections that keep us from being fruitful and bearing good works in Christ.

PRAYER. *Father, I praise You for Your constant pruning and continual nourishment.*

TO ABIDE in Christ means... to be always leaning on Him. —J.C. Ryle

APR. 10

...I believe in one Lord Jesus Christ...

REFLECTION. Jesus said that, unless we abide in Him and He in us, we cannot bear fruit (Jn 15:4-5).

We abide in Jesus by the choices we make. By obeying His commands, we allow Jesus to abide in us, filling us with the very life of God. This mutual indwelling is already a foretaste of heaven.

PRAYER. *Jesus, when I am weak and afraid, be my life and strength.*

CHRIST, the Good Shepherd, never loses track of His sheep. —J. I. Packer

APR. 11

...I believe in one Lord Jesus Christ...

REFLECTION. In contrast to false religious leaders, Jesus is "the Good Shepherd" (Jn 10:11). As shepherd, He guards, protects, and pastures us, providing for all our needs.

So evocative is this image of Jesus' role in our salvation that the earliest Christian art portrayed Jesus as a shepherd, even before depicting Him as crucified.

PRAYER. *Jesus, I trust You to number me always among Your fold.*

E FORESAW... my every sin..., nevertheless, fixed His heart upon me.

—A.W. Pink

APR. 12

...I believe in one Lord Jesus Christ...

REFLECTION. Jesus, the Good Shepherd, lays down His life for His sheep. He loves them more than His own life.

When the wolf comes, He defends them at the cost of His own life. Thus, when sin attacked our relationship with God, Jesus, the Good Shepherd, became the Lamb of God sacrificed for our salvation.

PRAYER. *Lamb of God, I thank You for wiping away my sins.*

NITY happens when we walk together.

—Pope Francis

APR. 13

...I believe in one Lord Jesus Christ...

REFLECTION. Jesus saw beyond the narrow confines of His own people. He spoke of other sheep whom He would lead to the one fold (Jn 10:16).

He now depends on us to draw closer to one another in truth and charity. When there are no divisions among us, others are attracted to follow the Good Shepherd.

PRAYER. *Good Shepherd, help me see all others as loved by You.*

HARITY...binds God with man and man with God. —St. Catherine of Siena

APR. 14

...I believe in one Lord Jesus Christ...

REFLECTION. Jesus prayed that we may be one as He and the Father are one (Jn 17:21).

As the Father and Son share all that they are with each other, we are called to be equally caring to others. The greater our love for others, the deeper our sharing in the very life of God.

PRAYER. *Jesus, through Your great love, grant me charity toward all.*

VERYTHING is nothing to me, but Jesus. —St. Bernadette

APR. 15

...I believe in one Lord Jesus Christ...

REFLECTION. Jesus is "the way, the truth and the life" (Jn 14:6). He stands apart from and above every other religious leader.

He is not just a teacher to heed, a leader to follow, or an example to imitate. As God, He is truth and life itself and, thus, the only perfect way to reach our eternal destiny.

PRAYER. *Jesus, in You I live, and move, and have my being.*

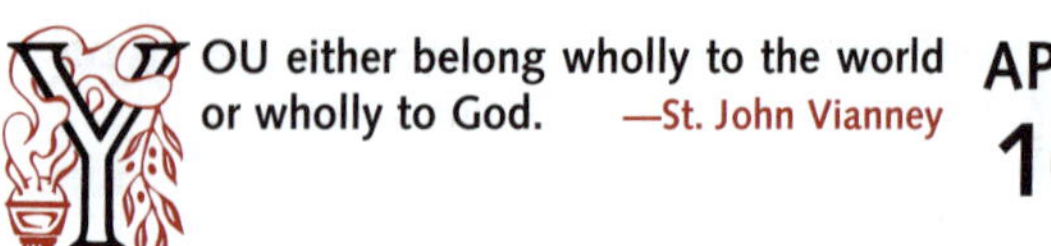

YOU either belong wholly to the world or wholly to God. —St. John Vianney

APR. 16

...I believe in one Lord Jesus Christ...

REFLECTION. By accepting Jesus as "the way, the truth and the life" (Jn 14:6), we make Him the standard for our choices.

Jesus, not the ever-changing ideologies of the day, shapes our lives. Living as Jesus teaches inevitably distances us from the world that places self over God. However, it truly enriches our lives.

PRAYER. *Jesus, I claim You as my God and my all.*

ONE of the most sincere forms of respect is listening to what another has to say. —Bryant H. McGill

APR. 17

...I believe in one Lord Jesus Christ...

REFLECTION. In Jesus' day, people addressed others as "Lord" (in Greek, *kyrios*) to show respect.

They especially used "Lord" for teachers with authority over their students or for masters able to command their servants. As our Teacher and our Master, Jesus the Lord deserves all our respect.

PRAYER. *Lord Jesus, help me always to heed Your word above every other.*

ESUS was God spelling himself out in language humanity could understand.
—S.D. Gordon

APR. 18

...I believe in one Lord Jesus Christ...

REFLECTION. The Septuagint, the Greek Old Testament, translates God's Hebrew name (Yahweh) as "Lord." The New Testament takes up this meaning, using "Lord" most frequently to express Jesus' divinity.

Thus, like the first Christians, we address Jesus as Lord because we acknowledge Jesus as truly God with divine authority over us and all creation.

PRAYER. *Jesus, You are my Lord and my God.*

ESUS Christ, Lord of all things! Possess all that I am—You alone. —St. Agatha

APR. 19

...I believe in one Lord Jesus Christ...

REFLECTION. Ancient Rome deified its emperors and made confessing the emperor as a god the bond uniting the entire Roman Empire. Christian martyrs refused to acclaim "Caesar is Lord."

Jesus alone was their Lord and God. Today, we cannot let anything or anyone take the place of Jesus as Lord in our lives.

PRAYER. *Lord Jesus, make me totally Yours.*

HOSE who refuse Him as Lord cannot use Him as Savior. —John MacArthur

APR. 20

...I believe in one Lord Jesus Christ...

REFLECTION. An angel announced to the shepherds the birth of Jesus as "a Savior who is Christ, the Lord" (Lk 2:11).

Jesus, the long-awaited Messiah, comes to save us from our sins. We can depend on His mercy as Savior to forgive our sins only if we welcome Him as the Lord whom we obey.

PRAYER. *To You, Jesus, I pledge my obedience today, tomorrow, and forever.*

ORSHIP is a lifestyle.
—Patrick Mabilog

APR. 21

...I believe in one Lord Jesus Christ...

REFLECTION. In Phil 2:5–11, Paul incorporates a hymn sung by the earliest Christians to proclaim Jesus as Lord.

The hymn extols Jesus who selflessly set aside His divine privileges to live as one of us to the point of death and thus was exalted as Lord. Only by imitating each day Jesus' selflessness do we truly worship Him as Lord.

PRAYER. *Gracious Lord, make me selfless like You in every way.*

NLESS Jesus is Lord of all, He is not Lord at all. —S.M. Zwemer

APR. 22

...I believe in one Lord Jesus Christ...

REFLECTION. The pagans believed in many gods, each lord of a limited sphere. But, as Paul asserts, there is but "one God, the Father... and one Lord, Jesus Christ" (1 Cor 8:6).

The Father who created all things through His Son has given Him rule over all creation. Jesus is Lord of all.

PRAYER. *Jesus, I surrender my life to You, my Lord and my God.*

HRIST existed as God before the ages; then He submitted to be born and become man. —St. Justin Martyr

APR. 23

...Jesus Christ, the Only Begotten Son of God...

REFLECTION. Although Jesus was born of Mary in time, God is His Father from all eternity.

The Greek word for "Only Begotten" (*monogenes*) stresses the fact that Jesus' relationship to the Father is unique. As Son, He existed with the Father before the world began.

PRAYER. *Jesus, out of love for us, You became one of us.*

E SENT the Word.... This is He who, being from everlasting, is today called the Son. —St. Polycarp

APR. 24

...born of the Father before all ages...

REFLECTION. In the fourth century, the heretic Arius taught that, before the Father created Him, the Son did not exist and, therefore, the Son is inferior to the Father.

However, there never was a moment when the Son did not exist. He is truly one with the Father, equal in glory.

PRAYER. *To You, Jesus, one with God, be everlasting praise.*

HE Father...has a Son; who also, being the first-begotten Word of God, is even God. —St. Justin Martyr

APR. 25

...born of the Father before all ages...

REFLECTION. This article of the Creed emphasizes that the Son came to be not by a physical but spiritual birth.

Just as the mind generates a thought or word and the two are one, so too the Father generates the Word and is one with the Word.

PRAYER. *Jesus, You are the eternal Word of God, living and true.*

HRIST is the God over all...
—St. Hippolytus

APR. 26

*...God from God, Light from Light,
true God from true God...*

REFLECTION. The Creed heaps these phrases together to state emphatically that Jesus who came as Messiah, lived among us, and taught us about God, is truly God Himself.

St. Paul expresses this truth when he says: "...we await our blessed hope...the appearance of the glory of our great God and Savior Jesus Christ" (Tit 2:13).

PRAYER. *Jesus, all glory be to You forever.*

OD is not distant: he is 'Emmanuel,' God-with-us...he has a face, the face of Jesus. —Pope Benedict XVI

APR. 27

*...God from God, Light from Light,
true God from true God...*

REFLECTION. The Creed sandwiches between two phrases virtually the same biblical metaphor of light for God.

The Scriptures refer to God as light (Ps 27:1) and identify Jesus as "the true light that enlightens everyone..." (Jn 1:9). Jesus is truly God among us.

PRAYER. *In You, Jesus, I encounter the one true God.*

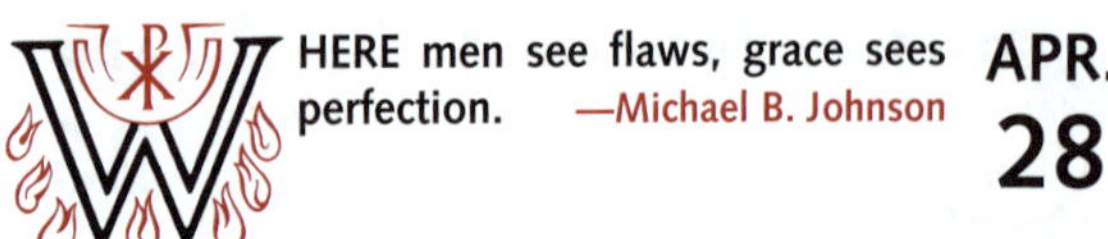

WHERE men see flaws, grace sees perfection. —Michael B. Johnson

APR. 28

...God from God, Light from Light, true God from true God...

REFLECTION. As the light of the sun keeps us from stumbling in the dark, Jesus, Light from Light, reveals all those obstacles along our way to heaven.

As the sun makes plants grow and flowers blossom, Jesus, true God, bathes us in divine grace, helping us produce the fruits of goodness and love.

PRAYER. *Lord Jesus, let Your light shine on me.*

ONE ray from His Heart can...make His flower bloom for eternity... —St. Thèrése of Lisieux

APR. 29

...God from God, Light from Light, true God from true God...

REFLECTION. "The sun, with all those planets... dependent on it can still ripen a bunch of grapes as if it had nothing else in the universe to do"(Galileo).

Likewise, Jesus, true God, pours out on us the Holy Spirit so that we may become what He has created us to be.

PRAYER. *Jesus, ready me for eternity with You.*

OD was in Christ reconciling the world to himself. —2 Cor 5:19

APR. 30

...begotten, not made...

REFLECTION. C.S. Lewis once said, "What God begets is God; just as what man begets is man. What God creates is not God, just as what man creates is not man."

Thus, *begotten, not made* means that Jesus our Savior is God, not a creature distinct from God. This technical language safeguards the truth that God Himself redeemed us.

PRAYER. *Jesus, make me at peace with God.*

ESUS replied...I and the Father are one. —Jn 10:30

MAY 1

...consubstantial with the Father...

REFLECTION. To combat the many false understandings of who Jesus truly is, the 4th century Council of Nicaea moved beyond the language of Scripture and coined the Greek philosophical word *homoousios* (consubstantial), meaning of the same substance.

With this one word, the Council summed up all those New Testament places where Jesus equates Himself with God.

PRAYER. *Lord Jesus, I thank You for showing me the Father.*

E MUST either worship Christ as God or despise or pity Him as man.

—John Gerstner

MAY 2

...consubstantial with the Father...

REFLECTION. Because Jesus claimed to be one with the Father, many Jews tried to stone Him to death.

They would not accept His word even on the basis of His many miracles (Jn 10:31-33). It takes faith to accept Jesus as God. And, it is believing Jesus is God that makes us Christian.

PRAYER. *Jesus, true God and true man, I offer You the worship of my life.*

HE Trinity is purely an object of faith... reason is too short to fathom this mystery but where reason cannot wade, there faith may swim.

—Thomas Watson

MAY 3

...consubstantial with the Father...

REFLECTION. In saving us, Jesus revealed Himself as one (consubstantial) with the Father and the Holy Spirit.

Because the Father acted in history, sending us His Son and the Holy Spirit, we know by faith the mystery of one God, three Persons.

PRAYER. *Increase my faith in You, three-in-one God.*

THERE is, therefore, one God, who by the Word and Wisdom created and arranged all things. —St. Irenaeus

MAY 4

...through him all things were made...

REFLECTION. Jesus is not a creature, inferior to God. As the Word of God, He is Creator along with the Father and the Holy Spirit.

Each person of the Trinity is involved in creation. As the fourth gospel proclaims, "the Word was God.... Through him all things came into existence" (Jn 1:1-3).

PRAYER. *Jesus, my Redeemer, I thank You for creating me.*

IN JESUS, the questions about identity, origin, meaning, purpose, and destiny are answered with a profound hope.

—Philip Wijaya

MAY 5

...through him all things were made...

REFLECTION. The Son of God became man at a point in time.

But from all eternity, as the Word of God, He has been active in creating and sustaining all of creation. Thus, we will only find the meaning of life itself when we look to Christ.

PRAYER. *Jesus, help me become what You created me to be.*

NOTHING...in the universe exists for its own sake.... Everything exists to make the greatness of Christ more fully known. —John Piper

MAY 6

...through him all things were made...

REFLECTION. Jesus is creation's ultimate destiny. "He is the image of the invisible God...all things were created through him and for him" (Col 1:15-16).

As the image of God, Jesus makes God known (Heb 1:3). Likewise, all creation exists to make Jesus known as God.

PRAYER. *Lord Jesus, make my life always mirror Your goodness.*

THE Father is still working, and I am at work as well. —Jn 5:17

MAY 7

...through him all things were made...

REFLECTION. Jesus, the eternal Son of God, is always active in creation.

From the immense galaxies to the smallest atom, from the battlefields that bloody our soil to the peaceful breeze refreshing the laborer, all are in His hands. He is most especially working in us, transforming us into His glory (2 Cor 3:18).

PRAYER. *Jesus, bring me to share Your glory.*

THE Son of God, who, on account of his surpassing love for his creation, endured to be born of the Virgin...

—St. Irenaeus

MAY 8

...For us men and for our salvation he came down from heaven...

REFLECTION. God created the world as good. Like Adam and Eve, we distort the goodness of all creation by our sins.

The Son of God came among us to reconcile us to God and restore the beauty of all creation.

PRAYER. *Mary our Mother, thank you for your son Jesus.*

WE CAN set no limits to the agency of the Redeemer to redeem...

—St. Clement of Alexandria

MAY 9

...For us men and for our salvation he came down from heaven...

REFLECTION. Written in Greek, the Creed uses the word *anthropos* for men.

This word means all people, men, women and children, born and unborn. The Son of God came for every one of us. As He loves all, so must we.

PRAYER. *Jesus, help me see everyone in the light of Your love.*

ICK, our nature demanded to be healed; fallen, to be raised up; dead, to rise again.... These things...moved God to descend to human nature.

—St. Gregory of Nyssa

MAY 10

...For us men and for our salvation he came down from heaven...

REFLECTION. By coming among us, the Son of God bridged the infinite distance between heaven and earth.

He descended to where we are so that we might ascend to where He is. Such great humility!

PRAYER. *Jesus, raise me up from my sins to be with You forever in heaven.*

E ARE saved by grace...for we can give God nothing in return for what he has bestowed on us.

—St. Jerome

MAY 11

...For us men and for our salvation he came down from heaven...

REFLECTION. Christ saves us by taking away our sin, restoring our friendship with God and giving us a share in the very life of the Trinity.

By the grace of the Holy Spirit we can respond in faith by living a holy life.

PRAYER. *In You, Jesus, is my salvation and the salvation of the whole world.*

THE grace of God has appeared bringing salvation... —Tit 2:11

MAY 12

...For us men and for our salvation he came down from heaven...

REFLECTION. Despite our best efforts, we cannot earn our salvation. Our salvation is pure grace.

It is a gift of God who loves us while we are yet sinners (Rom 5:8-10). In sending us His Son as our Savior, God Himself snatches us from the realm of Satan and from death.

PRAYER. *God, I am in awe of Your great love for me.*

IT IS by grace that you have been saved through faith. —Eph 2:8

MAY 13

...For us men and for our salvation he came down from heaven...

REFLECTION. Faith in Jesus opens us up to the grace of salvation. Faith is more than accepting Jesus' teachings.

It is believing who He is and entrusting our entire life to Him without reservation. With such faith, we accept His word, even when we do not completely understand it.

PRAYER. *In You, O Jesus, I place my faith in Your grace which is everywhere.*

JUST as a body is dead without a spirit, so faith without works is also dead.

—Jas 2:26

MAY 14

...For us men and for our salvation he came down from heaven...

REFLECTION. It is never enough simply to have faith in Jesus as Savior. The faith that saves is always accompanied by good works.

Our salvation is a continual process. Strengthened by God's grace, we avoid sin, grow in our love of God and produce good works.

PRAYER. *Savior God, give me true faith and the courage to always do good.*

GRACE is bestowed on us, not because we have done good works, but that we may be able to do them.

—St. Augustine

MAY 15

...For us men and for our salvation he came down from heaven...

REFLECTION. So complete is our salvation in Christ that, as Paul teaches, both our very desire and our ability to do good come from God's grace (Phil 2:13).

For this reason, we can have hope in any struggle or temptation and do what is right and just in God's eyes.

PRAYER. *O God, Your grace is sufficient for me.*

N HIM it pleased God...to reconcile all things...whether on earth or in heaven...
—Col 1:19-20

MAY 16

...For us men and for our salvation he came down from heaven...

REFLECTION. Adam and Eve's fall from grace affected all of creation (Rom 5:12). Thus, Christ came not just to save us.

He came to redeem the world. Trusting in Him, with great eagerness, "we await the promised new heaven and new earth..." (2 Pet 3:13).

PRAYER. *Lord, keep me eyes fixed on the glory yet to come.*

E ARE co-redeemers of the world
—St. Teresa of the Andes

MAY 17

...For us men and for our salvation he came down from heaven...

REFLECTION. St. Augustine tells us that "God created us without us, but he did not will to save us without us."

Gifted with freedom, we cooperate with Jesus in our own salvation. By living as faithful members of His Body, the Church, we also cooperate with Him in the salvation of others.

PRAYER. *Jesus, our Redeemer help me always cooperate with You.*

HE worst thing in the world is not sin; it is the denial of sin.

—Venerable Fulton Sheen

MAY 18

...For us men and for our salvation he came down from heaven...

REFLECTION. While the world would convince us that we are basically good people with a few imperfections, the Scriptures teach that "all have sinned and fallen short of the glory of God" (Rom 3:23).

Only by acknowledging our sins can we claim Jesus as Savior.

PRAYER. *Jesus, have mercy on me, a sinner.*

OTHING is so strong as gentleness, nothing so gentle as real strength.

—St. Francis de Sales

MAY 19

...For us men and for our salvation he came down from heaven...

REFLECTION. Jesus gently entered our world in a manger as Savior and gently left it riding on a donkey.

When the sons of Zebedee wanted to call down fire from heaven on the inhospitable Samaritans, He refused (Lk 9:54). His gentleness is the strength of His love.

PRAYER. *Jesus, gentle of heart, make my heart like Yours.*

OUR Lord's patience means salvation.
—2 Pet 3:15

MAY 20

...For us men and for our salvation he came down from heaven...

REFLECTION. God wills all to be saved. We rebel against Him by our sins. Yet, He remains patient with us.

He gives us Jesus as our Savior. No matter how sinful we are, Jesus never gives up on us. As Paul teaches, Jesus' patience with us sinners is "inexhaustible" (1 Tim 1:16).

PRAYER. *Lord, lead us by Your endless patience to repentance.*

IN THE Incarnation the whole human race recovers the dignity of the image of God.
—Dietrich Bonhoeffer

MAY 21

...by the Holy Spirit was incarnate of the Virgin Mary...

REFLECTION. The eternal Son of God took on our human nature.

Jesus remains a divine person, uniting in Himself a divine and human nature. This mystery of the Incarnation makes us reflect more perfectly God's own image and likeness.

PRAYER. *By Your Incarnation, O Jesus, help us to value the gift of our humanity.*

E TAKES on the poverty of my flesh, that I may gain the riches of his divinity.
—St. Gregory of Nazianzus

MAY 22

...by the Holy Spirit was incarnate of the Virgin Mary...

REFLECTION. In taking on our flesh and blood, the Son of God clothes our lowliness with His splendor, our weakness with His strength, our death with His life.

Because of the Incarnation, we rise up from the material world to the heavenly.

PRAYER. *Jesus, by Your Incarnation, grant us everlasting life.*

OD is waiting to be found everywhere.
—S. Niequist

MAY 23

...by the Holy Spirit was incarnate of the Virgin Mary...

REFLECTION. By the Incarnation, the Son of God became fully human.

He did not abandon His divine nature, but lived our human life with all its hopes and disappointments, all its pains and sorrows. Thus, He sanctified all of life, enabling us to find God in every experience of our lives.

PRAYER. *Lord, help me see You in the events of my everyday life.*

HE world is charged with the grandeur of God. —Gerard Manley Hopkins

MAY 24

...by the Holy Spirit was incarnate of the Virgin Mary...

REFLECTION. The Incarnation is not an afterthought in the mind of the Creator.

From the very beginning, God ordered material creation to the coming of man and ultimately to the coming of the Son. God's saving plan includes the world's physical reality as good.

PRAYER. *By the mystery of Your Incarnation, fill me with wonder at creation's goodness.*

HE Word became flesh... and we saw his glory...full of grace and truth. —Jn 1:14

MAY 25

...by the Holy Spirit was incarnate of the Virgin Mary...

REFLECTION. In the Incarnation, God's compassion is fully revealed.

Jesus, the Divine Physician, heals those broken in body and spirit with the touch of His hand. He embraces the sinner with His tender love. He teaches those searching for truth with the words of His mouth.

PRAYER. *In You, O Jesus, we touch the heart of God.*

FOR as without woman Adam produced woman, so did the Virgin without man... bring forth a man. —St. John Chrysostom

MAY 26

...by the Holy Spirit was incarnate of the Virgin Mary...

REFLECTION. In the Incarnation, God accomplishes what no man could do. He brought forth creation from nothing.

Likewise, from the empty, barren womb of the Virgin Mary, He brings forth His Son in the flesh.

PRAYER. *To You, Lord Jesus, who are the beginning of the New Creation, be all praise and honor.*

THOUGH heaven be God's palace, yet it is not his prison. —Thomas Brooks

MAY 27

...by the Holy Spirit was incarnate of the Virgin Mary...

REFLECTION. The angel Gabriel announced the Baptist's birth to Zechariah in the Temple in Jerusalem (Lk 1:11-13). But, he announced Jesus' birth to Mary in Nazareth (Lk 1:26-27).

Not in a religious setting, but in an ordinary home, the Son of God becomes man. Thus, we can encounter Him wherever we are.

PRAYER. *Jesus, by Your Incarnation, You make holy wherever I am.*

GOD became human, truly human out of his own grace. —Karl Barth

MAY 28

...by the Holy Spirit was incarnate of the Virgin Mary...

REFLECTION. The Holy Spirit overshadows Mary and, by His power, she conceives our Savior. Salvation comes to us not because of any human initiative or action.

Joseph does nothing. Mary does nothing. God does it all by the power of the Holy Spirit. Our salvation comes from God's initiative.

PRAYER. *Jesus, Son of the Virgin, save me by Your amazing grace.*

THE Son of God became man...only in Mary and through Mary.

—St. Louis Marie de Montfort

MAY 29

...by the Holy Spirit was incarnate of the Virgin Mary...

REFLECTION. The Son of God took a human nature from Mary by the action of the Holy Spirit.

The Virgin birth of Jesus is an unmistakable sign that Jesus, eternally begotten of the Father, has Mary as His mother on earth, but God as His Father in heaven.

PRAYER. *Jesus, You are truly a divine person.*

OMAN! above all women glorified, Our tainted nature's solitary boast... —Wadsworth

MAY 30

...by the Holy Spirit was incarnate of the Virgin Mary...

REFLECTION. At the Annunciation, the angel Gabriel greeted Mary, saying, "Hail, full of grace" (Lk 1:28).

Unlike any of Adam and Eve's descendants, God preserved Mary from all sin from the first moment of her conception. He filled her with His grace in order to prepare her to be the Mother of the Savior.

PRAYER. *O Mary conceived without sin, pray for us.*

Y DIVINE power a Virgin conceived, a Virgin bore, and Virgin she remained. —Pope St. Leo the Great

MAY 31

...by the Holy Spirit was incarnate of the Virgin Mary...

REFLECTION. After Jesus' birth, Mary remained a virgin. She totally consecrated her entire self to God, single-mindedly giving herself for His service.

She herself became a sign of the world to come where there is no marriage (Mt 22:30).

PRAYER. *Through the intercession of Mary ever-virgin, Lord, help me give myself to You completely.*

ARY, a Virgin not only undefiled but a Virgin whom grace has made inviolate, free of every stain of sin.

—St. Ambrose

JUNE 1

...by the Holy Spirit was incarnate of the Virgin Mary...

REFLECTION. Mary who bore the Savior was herself saved by Him in a unique way befitting her role in our redemption.

By the foreseen merits of Jesus our Redeemer, God gave her the grace never to sin. Her unique holiness is totally God's gift.

PRAYER. *Mary most pure, pray for me.*

EATH came through Eve, but life has come through Mary. —St. Jerome

JUNE 2

...by the Holy Spirit was incarnate of the Virgin Mary...

REFLECTION. Eve was joined to Adam in disobeying God and bringing death to the world.

However, Mary was always united with Jesus in obeying God. At the Annunciation, her obedience opened the way for Jesus to enter the world. Her obedience ultimately brings life. She is the New Eve.

PRAYER. *Mary, Mother of all the living, pray that I, too, may obey God.*

ARY is an example to the faithful... worthy of imitation because she is the first and most perfect of Christ's disciples. —Pope St. Paul VI

JUNE 3

...by the Holy Spirit was incarnate of the Virgin Mary...

REFLECTION. At the Visitation, Elizabeth praised Mary, because she believed what the angel had told her about the Son she would deliver (Lk 1:45).

Thus, Mary, not hesitating to believe in Jesus as the long-awaited Messiah, became the very first disciple.

PRAYER. *Lord, help me believe as Mary did.*

OD gives...sufficient grace...to know His holy will, and to do it fully. —St. Ignatius of Loyola

JUNE 4

...by the Holy Spirit was incarnate of the Virgin Mary...

REFLECTION. When Mary presented Jesus in the Temple forty days after His birth, Simeon confirmed the angel's message to her.

Then he prophesied Jesus' sufferings as Messiah. He also predicted that Mary would share in Jesus' sufferings (Lk 2:33-35). Only gradually did Mary come to understand fully her vocation as the Mother of Jesus.

PRAYER. *Mary, help me know God's will for me.*

THE conscious water saw its God and blushed. —R. Crashaw

JUNE 5

...by the Holy Spirit was incarnate of the Virgin Mary...

REFLECTION. Before seeing Jesus work a single miracle, Mary believed in Him. At the wedding at Cana, Mary tells Jesus that the wine ran out, trusting He could do something (Jn 2:3).

Faith is believing before seeing. Responding to Mary's intercession, Jesus performs His first miracle, changing water into wine, thus revealing His glory as God.

PRAYER. *Lord, help me believe in Your power to do good even before I see it.*

MOTHERS hold their children's hands for a short while, but their hearts forever. —Author Unknown

JUNE 6

...by the Holy Spirit was incarnate of the Virgin Mary...

REFLECTION. Although Mary resided at Nazareth during Jesus' public ministry, she remained united with Him by a close maternal bond.

She followed His every step. She even sought Him out when concerned that He was expending Himself too much. In Mary, we see the true heart of a mother.

PRAYER. *Immaculate Heart of Mary, pray for all mothers.*

ARY...offers Jesus, gives him over, and begets him to the end for our sake. —Pope St. John Paul II

JUNE 7

...by the Holy Spirit was incarnate of the Virgin Mary...

REFLECTION. At the crucifixion, the apostles fled. However, the women who had accompanied Jesus in His ministry remained with Jesus to the end.

Love is the soul of fidelity. Loyalty endures the test of suffering. And the most loyal of all was Jesus' own mother. His sufferings were hers.

PRAYER. *Mary, Mother of Sorrows, be my consolation in times of suffering.*

OGETHER they accomplished the task of man's redemption...both offered up one and the same sacrifice to God: she in the blood of her heart, he in the blood of the flesh...—Arnold of Chartres

JUNE 8

...by the Holy Spirit was incarnate of the Virgin Mary...

REFLECTION. On Calvary, Mary uniquely cooperates in our salvation as Co-Redemptrix.

With Jesus, she offered the Father the Body and Blood Jesus received from her spotless womb.

PRAYER. *Mary, help me join Jesus in His work of redemption.*

THERE can be no point of contact between Absolute Deity and Fallen Humanity except through Jesus...

—Charles Spurgeon

JUNE 9

...and became man...

REFLECTION. While not abandoning His divinity, God the Son became man.

This unfathomable mystery of the Incarnation means that Christ is a divine person with a divine nature and a human nature. Uniting the two natures in Himself without confusion or commingling, He is truly the one Mediator between God and man.

PRAYER. *Jesus, in You, I can approach God Himself and know His unfailing love.*

A GOD who became so small could only be mercy and love.

—St. Thérése of Lisieux

JUNE 10

...and became man...

REFLECTION. The Son of God was born as a helpless infant, totally dependent on His parents. Omnipotence became weakness for love of us.

He humbled Himself in this way so that He could take on our human condition from birth to death. No part of our life experience is unknown to Him.

PRAYER. *Jesus, by the mystery of Your birth, grant me true humility.*

HE kingdom of God is righteousness and peace. —Zac Poonen

JUNE 11

...and became man...

REFLECTION. The Roman emperor Caesar Augustus ended generations of bloodshed and war and established the *Pax Romana.*

The Romans praised his birth as heralding peace for their nation. During the time of Caesar Augustus, Jesus was born. As the angel announced to the shepherds, Jesus came to bring peace to every nation. Only in Jesus can we find true peace.

PRAYER. *Protect innocent victims of war, and grant peace, O Lord, in our day.*

HE hinge of history is on the door of a Bethlehem stable. —Ralph W. Sockman

JUNE 12

...and became man...

REFLECTION. At the time of Jesus' birth in Bethlehem, there were shepherds in the surrounding fields tending sheep destined for sacrifice in the Temple.

All those sacrifices would soon end. History has a new beginning in Jesus, the spotless Lamb of God, the perfect Victim who offers the perfect sacrifice for the sins of the world.

PRAYER. *Lamb of God, take away all my sins.*

THE Eucharist began at Bethlehem in Mary's arms.... She...brought to humanity the Bread for which it was famishing... —St. Peter Julian Eymard

JUNE 13

...and became man...

REFLECTION. Bethlehem is located in the rich grain-producing region of Old Testament times. In fact, "Bethlehem" literally means "House of Bread." How appropriate that Jesus is born in Bethlehem.

He comes as the true Bread of life to satisfy our deepest hungers.

PRAYER. *O Lord Jesus, help me always turn to You for my deepest needs and longings.*

IN HIS former advent, He was wrapped in swaddling clothes in the manger; in His second, He covers Himself with light as with a garment. —St. Cyril of Jerusalem

JUNE 14

...and became man...

REFLECTION. To protect her newborn son, Mary wrapped Jesus in swaddling clothes.

Likewise, at His burial, He is wrapped in linen cloths. Yet, He who took on our frail humanity leaves behind His burial clothes, raising us up to share His Divinity.

PRAYER. *Jesus, grant Your strength to my weakness.*

HE Son of God was circumcised in the flesh...that we might be circumcised in spirit. —St. Thomas Aquinas

JUNE 15

...and became man...

REFLECTION. Eight days after His birth, Jesus was circumcised according to Jewish custom, enrolling Him as a member of the Chosen People.

From the very beginning, Jesus shows us the importance of our body in the economy of salvation. Jesus comes to redeem all that we are, body and soul.

PRAYER. *Jesus, by Your grace, grant me health in body and soul,*

OR our sake He was presented to the Lord that we may learn to offer ourselves to God. —St Thomas Aquinas

JUNE 16

...and became man...

REFLECTION. In obedience to the Mosaic Law, Mary and Joseph present Jesus in the Temple in Jerusalem forty days after His birth (Lk 2:22).

Their meticulous obedience of the Law is the school in which Jesus in His human nature learns the virtue of obedience. Parents' good example is irreplaceable.

PRAYER. *Teach me, Lord Jesus, to offer myself to God to do with me as He chooses.*

OPE is the beacon that shines in the darkness, reminding us of God's love.

—St. Bonaventure

JUNE 17

...and became man...

REFLECTION. When the infant Jesus is presented in the Temple, Simeon and Anna appear on the scene. Both, advanced in years, were awaiting "the consolation of Israel" (Lk 2:25).

Moved by the Holy Spirit, each proclaims Him the fulfillment of God's promises. They represent all those who, despite the passing years, never lose hope in God.

PRAYER. *Lord, strengthen my hope in You and in Your perfect plan for me.*

IKE a traveler who reaches the end of his journey, I'll be falling into God's arms!

—St. Thérèse of Lisieux

JUNE 18

...and became man...

REFLECTION. When Simeon met the child Jesus in the Temple, "he took him in his arms ..." (Lk 2:28). He is aptly called "*Theodochus*" or "the God-receiver."

Embracing Jesus who brings salvation, the aged Simeon is not afraid of death. He utters his *Nunc Dimittis*. He is at peace because salvation has come.

PRAYER. *Jesus, hold me close to You and never let go!*

RAYER should be the key of the day and the lock of the night. —George Herbert

JUNE 19

...and became man...

REFLECTION. At the Presentation in the Temple, the elderly Anna, the only prophetess named in the New Testament, recognizes Jesus as the Messiah and praises God.

Her unceasing prayer day and night in the Temple prepared her for this moment. Prayer opens our eyes to see God in our lives and our lips to praise Him.

PRAYER. *Lord, increase our desire to pray without ceasing.*

HEREVER his light leads, we follow. —Emmanuel Onimisi

JUNE 20

...and became man...

REFLECTION. By a star, God led the magi, wise men steeped in science, to find Christ.

First, by nature's dim light, God led them to Jerusalem. Then, by the bright light of Sacred Scripture, He brought them to Bethlehem. Following God's light, they find the Child and acknowledge their God. God is always leading us to discover His Presence among us.

PRAYER. *Lord, help me always to seek You and find You.*

EROD...you would rule more happily yourself, if you were to submit to His command... —Pope St. Leo the Great

JUNE 21

...and became man...

REFLECTION. In Jesus, God came to save the world. But, the world did not welcome His coming. Herod, afraid to lose his power, tried to kill Jesus.

In Herod is already anticipated the response of all those who reject Christ because they hold too firmly to this world.

PRAYER. *Lord Jesus, You alone are worthy of my obedience.*

HRIST fled into Egypt [to] teach us... as exiles on the earth [to]...strive for heaven as our true country. —Cornelius a Lapide

JUNE 22

...and became man...

REFLECTION. Not knowing where the Christ child is, King Herod slaughters innocent children in an attempt to kill Him.

But, the Holy Family escapes his murderous wrath by fleeing to Egypt. Becoming one with us does not exempt the Son of God from the dangers of this life.

PRAYER. *Jesus, keep my eyes focused on my true home. Protect me on the journey.*

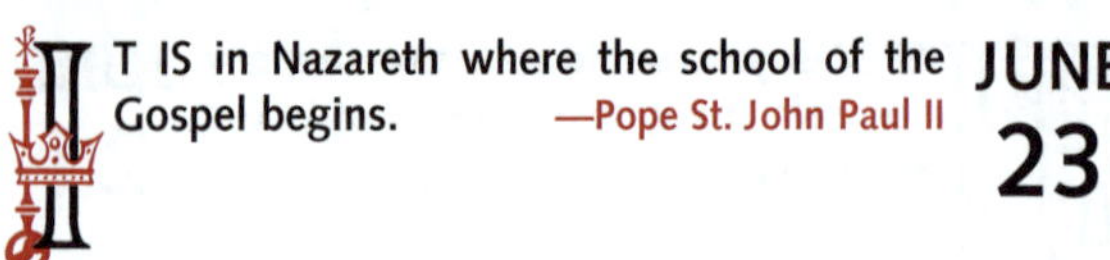

IT IS in Nazareth where the school of the Gospel begins. —Pope St. John Paul II

JUNE 23

...and became man...

REFLECTION. As a child, Jesus lived in Nazareth, a village nestled in the rolling hills of Galilee.

In this small community of tightly knit families, Jesus grew up in the traditions of the Jewish faith. In His family life in Nazareth, He learned in His human nature the obedience that led Him to the Cross.

PRAYER. *Jesus, help me cherish family life by my prayers and actions.*

LOVE God, serve God; everything is in that. —St. Clare of Assisi

JUNE 24

...and became man...

REFLECTION. Even as a teenager, Jesus was well aware of who He was.

When Mary and Joseph find Him in the Temple after three days' absence, He responds, "Did you not know that I must be in my Father's house?" (Lk 2:49). As the Son of God, Jesus is totally dedicated to the work of His Father.

PRAYER. *Loving Jesus, help me do God's will in all things.*

ESUS...has become what we are, in order that He may make us entirely what He is.

—St. Irenaeus of Lyons

JUNE 25

...and became man...

REFLECTION. Jesus began His public ministry by receiving the baptism of John the Baptist.

He joined the crowds flocking to John at the Jordan to receive a baptism signifying their turning from sin to God. Jesus, though sinless, submitted to this baptism to identify with every sinner He had come to save.

PRAYER. *Jesus, make me detest all sin but never to hate the sinner.*

HE secret to joy is to keep seeking God...

—Ann Voskamp

JUNE 26

...and became man...

REFLECTION. Many accepted baptism from John the Baptist, because they heard in his preaching the very voice of God.

They were eager to find God. By being baptized with them in the Jordan, Jesus, who came to find the lost, took to Himself the pain of all those who seek to find God.

PRAYER. *Lord Jesus, help me always to seek and find God even in my darkest struggles.*

THE Kingdom of God is present wherever Jesus is king. —Rick Warren

JUNE 27

...and became man...

REFLECTION. John the Baptist preached his baptism as the preparation for the imminent coming of the Kingdom of God.

Jesus received John's baptism to prepare Himself as the one who was ushering in that long-desired kingdom. Jesus had come to understand this was His Messianic mission.

PRAYER. *Jesus, I give my life to You completely so that I may live each day within the everlasting Kingdom of God.*

GOD invites us to join with him...to enter...his love. —Pope Benedict XVI

JUNE 28

...and became man...

REFLECTION. Mark tells us that, at Jesus' Baptism, the heavens *were ripped open* (Mk 1:10). Using the same word, Mark says that, the veil in the Temple *was ripped open* at the moment of Jesus' death (Mk 15:38).

In Jesus, the separation between heaven and earth, between us and God, no longer exists. God freely communicates with us.

PRAYER. *Jesus, help me always respond to God's love.*

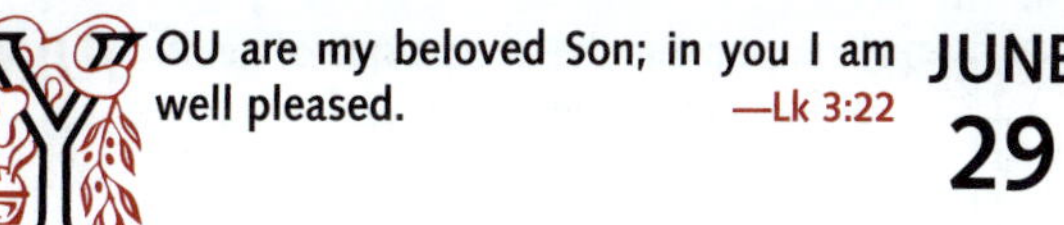

YOU are my beloved Son; in you I am well pleased. —Lk 3:22

JUNE 29

...and became man...

REFLECTION. During His hidden years, Jesus discerned the Father's will. Understanding what His mission was, Jesus descended into the waters of the Jordan with all those longing for salvation.

Ascending from those waters, the Father assured Him that He indeed was the One He sent to save us. This was the appointed moment for Jesus to begin His work.

PRAYER. *Jesus, teach me to be wise and to trust in the mission You give me in life.*

THIS is He who, after the manner of a dove, when our Lord was baptized, came and abode upon Him, dwelling in Christ full and entire...so that from Him others might receive some enjoyment of His graces. —Novatian

JUNE 30

...and became man...

REFLECTION. As Jesus came up out of the waters of the Jordan, the Holy Spirit who sanctified Him at conception came down upon Him to equip Him for His public ministry.

PRAYER. *Lord Jesus, graciously pour out upon me the gift of Your Holy Spirit.*

HE Baptism is the acceptance of death for the sins of humanity.

—Pope Benedict XVI

JULY 1

...and became man...

REFLECTION. At Jesus' baptism, the Father says to Him, "in you I am well pleased" (Lk 3:22).

Echoing Isaiah's description of the Suffering Servant who dies for the people's iniquities (Isa 53), these words indicate that Jesus will die for our sins. Receiving baptism, Jesus accepts God's plan for our salvation. Jordan anticipates Calvary.

PRAYER. *Jesus, in You my sins are washed away and I become a child of God.*

NE of the best results of temptation is that it shows us what is in our hearts.

—A. B. Simpson

JULY 2

...and became man...

REFLECTION. After the Father anointed Jesus with the Holy Spirit at His baptism for His work as Messiah, Jesus immediately goes into the desert.

There, in combat with Satan, He decides to accomplish His mission not according to popular expectations, but according to God's will.

PRAYER. *In all my struggles with temptation, direct my heart in Your ways, O Lord.*

ORN of the Virgin Mary, He has truly been made one of us, like us in all things except sin (Heb 4:15).

—Gaudium et Spes, 23

JULY 3

...and became man...

REFLECTION. The Son of God took on our flesh, completely sharing in our humanity.

In the desert, the devil truly tempted Him repeatedly to put His own comfort over the sufferings He was to endure for our salvation. But Jesus resisted, not committing a single sin.

PRAYER. *Strengthen me, Lord, to resist Satan and all evil spirits.*

EMPTATION is Satan's weapon to defeat us, but...God's tool to build us.

—Warren Wiersbe

JULY 4

...and became man...

REFLECTION. The Holy Spirit led Jesus into the desert to be tempted (Mk 1:12). God did not allow Jesus to be tempted so that He would weaken and succumb to evil.

Rather, He permitted the devil to tempt Him so that Jesus would be strengthened in His resolve to do the Father's will in all things.

PRAYER. *Jesus, lead me always by the Holy Spirit to avoid sin.*

E...TOOK on our temptations, burdened himself with our wretchedness in order to defeat the Evil One and open a path to God for us...

—Pope Benedict XVI

JULY 5

...and became man...

REFLECTION. In every temptation we face, there is some enticement to decide on our own what is right and wrong, putting ourselves in God's place.

In the desert, Jesus kept God at the center of His life. That was the secret of His victory over evil.

PRAYER. *By Your grace, help me, O Lord, overcome every temptation to sin.*

AN does not live by bread alone, but by every word that comes forth from the mouth of God. **—Mt 4:4**

JULY 6

...and became man...

REFLECTION. The devil approaches Jesus who has been fasting for a long time. He tempts Him to turn stones into bread.

But Jesus refuses to make His physical needs His priority. Jesus sees beyond the materialism of this world. Our deepest hunger only God can satisfy.

PRAYER. *You alone, O God, are the answer to my deepest hungers.*

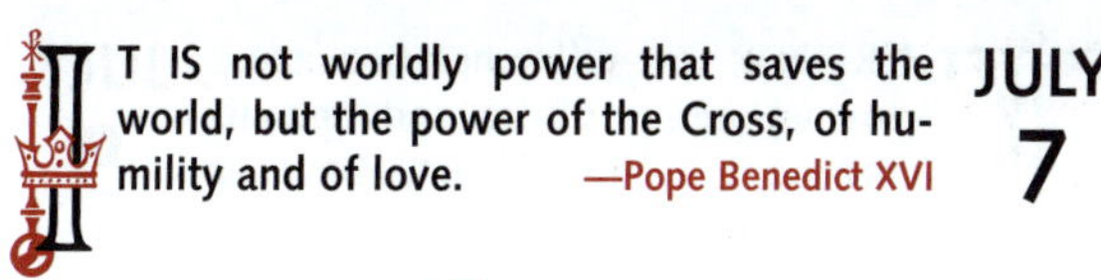

IT IS not worldly power that saves the world, but the power of the Cross, of humility and of love. —Pope Benedict XVI

JULY 7

...and became man...

REFLECTION. In the second temptation, Satan tells Jesus to throw Himself down from the Temple, forcing God to protect Him with angels. Jesus refuses to use His divine power to dazzle the eyes of spectators (Mt 4:5-7).

He came to convert our hearts to God, not to win passing acclaim.

PRAYER. *Jesus, open my heart to God's love so that I may always choose the good.*

IF WE ever forget that we are One Nation Under God, then we will be a nation gone under. —Ronald Reagan

JULY 8

...and became man...

REFLECTION. Jesus came to establish God's kingdom on earth.

In a third temptation, Satan offers to give Jesus a quick way to attain the political power of all the world's kingdoms if Jesus bows down to him (Mt 4:9-10). Jesus refuses. Only by submitting to God's authority can any kingdom last.

PRAYER. *God, You alone will I worship and adore forever.*

THERE is a vast difference between... knowing about Christ and actually knowing Him—the difference between heaven and hell. —Steven J Lawson

JULY 9

...and became man...

REFLECTION. Satan tried desperately to get Jesus to do something extraordinary.

No other individual would be tempted to change stones to bread, believe that He had angels at His command or aspire to world dominion. Even the devil recognized that Jesus was no ordinary man, but someone possessing incredible powers.

PRAYER. *Jesus, help me to truly know You and obey You.*

JESUS [was] fully aware that...he had come from God and was returning to God... —Jn 13:3

JULY 10

...and became man...

REFLECTION. Satan tried to get Jesus to distrust His own self-awareness. He repeated again and again, "If you are the Son of God" (Mt 4:3, 5), then you can do what I ask.

However, Jesus refused to work miracles to prove who He was. He knew He was God's Son sent to save others.

PRAYER. *Jesus, help me know my true identity.*

THE Word of God is a lamp by night, a light by day, and a delight at all times.
—Charles Spurgeon

JULY 11

...and became man...

REFLECTION. Jesus resisted Satan in the desert with citations from Deuteronomy (6:13; 6:16; 8:3). Jesus thoroughly knew the Hebrew Scriptures and found strength and direction in them for His life.

We should never underestimate the power of God's Word to inspire us and get us through life's difficult moments.

PRAYER. *Make me live in Your Word, O Lord.*

IF GOD were not my friend, Satan would not be so much my enemy. —Thomas Brooks

JULY 12

...and became man...

REFLECTION. After tempting Jesus in the desert, the devil left Him only for a time (Lk 4:13).

The devil attacked Jesus throughout His entire life. In Peter's objection to the Cross (Mt 16:23) and in Judas' betrayal (Lk 22:3), Jesus recognized the hand of Satan. Because He was so holy, Jesus constantly battled Satan.

PRAYER. *I trust You, Jesus, to make me strong in resisting evil.*

LIFE without prayer is a life without power. —Edwin Harvey

JULY 13

...and became man...

REFLECTION. At the beginning of His ministry, Jesus went alone into the desert to be tempted by the devil.

At the end of His ministry, He withdrew to be alone in the Garden of Gethsemane to struggle with the temptation to abandon the way of the cross. As a man, Jesus found His strength to overcome all temptations in prayer. And so must we.

PRAYER. *Lord, increase my desire to pray.*

NCE sin is overcome, and man's harmony with God restored, creation is reconciled, too. —Pope Benedict XVI

JULY 14

...and became man...

REFLECTION. When Adam and Eve succumbed to Satan's temptation, all creation suffered. The ground became hard to work. Beasts became hostile.

After overcoming Satan's temptations in the desert, Jesus was at peace with the wild beasts and the angels (Mk 1:13). In conquering evil, Jesus restores creation to its original innocence and harmony.

PRAYER. *Jesus, in Your victory over sin is lasting peace.*

EARNING is a lifelong process...
—Peter Drucker

JULY
15

...and became man...

REFLECTION. As a man, Jesus was misunderstood. When Mary and Joseph found Jesus in the temple, they did not understand His words that He had to be in His Father's house (Lk 2:49-50).

If those closest to Jesus found it difficult to comprehend His words, we should not be surprised at our need to reflect deeply on Jesus' words.

PRAYER. *Jesus, inspire me with a greater and greater desire to know You better each day.*

INDNESS causes misunderstanding...to evaporate.
—Albert Schweitzer

JULY
16

...and became man...

REFLECTION. Jesus was the perfect teacher. But His disciples were not the perfect students.

For example, when He warned them about the hypocrisy and bad influence of the Pharisees and Herod (Mk 8:15-16), they were confused. Jesus remained calm; and, with great kindness, He led them by questions to understand His words. Jesus does not give up on slow learners.

PRAYER. *Jesus, patiently lead me to heed all Your warnings against evil.*

WISDOM is the hallmark of the humble. —Prov 11:2

JULY 17

...and became man...

REFLECTION. After Jesus taught the parable of the Sower and the Seed, the disciples did not understand what Jesus was saying.

Privately they asked Him to explain it to them (Lk 8:4-9). They were humble enough not to let their lack of understanding keep them from the truth. When we honestly acknowledge our ignorance, we are truly wise.

PRAYER. *Lord Jesus, You alone are the source of true wisdom and knowledge.*

JESUS is the genuine newness which surpasses all human expectations. —Pope St. John Paul II

JULY 18

...and became man...

REFLECTION. When Jesus calmed the raging storm at sea with a single command, the disciples questioned, "Who can this be? Even the wind and sea obey him" (Mk 4:41).

They saw a man before them; yet, they experienced in Him the power of God. As for them, so for us: Jesus is always more than we imagine.

PRAYER. *Jesus, You are my peace and sure refuge at all times.*

HE cross is the only way of salvation.
—Billy Graham

JULY 19

...and became man...

REFLECTION. After Peter confessed Jesus as the Messiah, Jesus began to predict that, as Messiah, He would suffer and die.

The disciples who were expecting a powerful Messiah to overthrow Rome could not understand. Peter even rebuked Jesus for thinking of death on the cross (Mt 16:13-24). It is human to shrink from suffering. Yet, Jesus endured the cross, loving us to the end.

PRAYER. *Lord, by Your Cross, save me.*

UMILITY is not thinking less of yourself, it's thinking of yourself less.
—Rick Warren

JULY 20

...and became man...

REFLECTION. So much did the disciples misunderstand Jesus as the Messiah that James and John actually asked Jesus for the seats of honor when He established His political kingdom on earth (Mk 10:37).

They did not understand Jesus' teaching and ministry of humble service. We truly understand Jesus when, like Him, we put the good of others first.

PRAYER. *Jesus, may I do all to honor You.*

ESUS knew that on this side of eternity that people are imperfect. —Brian Chilton

JULY 21

...and became man...

REFLECTION. The other disciples become angry when James and John request the place of honor in Jesus' kingdom (Mk 10:41).

They wanted those places for themselves. All the disciples brought sorrow to the human heart of Jesus for not understanding His teaching. Yet, despite their repeated misunderstandings, Jesus keeps them as His disciples.

PRAYER. *Lord, hold me close even when I fail to understand You.*

E ALLOWED them to taste for a short time contemplation of eternal joy, so that they might bear persecution bravely. —St. Bede

JULY 22

...and became man...

REFLECTION. In the Transfiguration, Jesus revealed the glory of His divinity to Peter, James and John.

Seeing Jesus' glory, the disciples misunderstood. Peter mistakenly suggested setting up camp for Jesus, Moses and Elijah so that Jesus could establish His kingdom with His divine power without the Cross (Lk 9:33).

PRAYER. *Jesus, help me embrace the Cross.*

EAR makes us feel our humanity.
—Benjamin Disraeli

JULY 23

...and became man...

REFLECTION. When Jesus told His disciples of His upcoming death, "they did not understand what he was saying and they were afraid to ask him about it" (Mk 9:32).

Jesus' prediction so completely demolished their hopes of a militant Messiah that they were afraid even to question Him. Fear of losing our cherished opinions can block our minds from truth.

PRAYER. *Lord, move me beyond my human fears to embrace Your teaching.*

HE worst distance between two people is misunderstanding. **—N. Dixit**

JULY 24

...and became man...

REFLECTION. Jesus' Palm Sunday entry into Jerusalem caused confusion, not comprehension. Jesus accepted the acclaim of the crowds as the awaited conquering King of Israel.

Yet, He enters on a gentle donkey, not triumphantly on a horse. Even at the end of His life, "his disciples did not understand this" (Jn 12:16). Their expectations distance them from Jesus.

PRAYER. *Jesus, dispel my false hopes and draw me to Your side.*

HE Pharisees...immediately began to plot with the Herodians how they might put him to death. —Mk 3:6

JULY 25

...and became man...

REFLECTION. As a man, Jesus faced hostility and opposition. Because He placed the good of the individual over man-made religious rules, He healed on the Sabbath.

As a result, from the very beginning of His ministry, those who scrupulously kept the Sabbath turned against Him.

PRAYER. *Jesus, grant me courage always to do what pleases God.*

HE scribes and the Pharisees watched him closely... so that they would have a charge to bring against him. —Lk 6:7

JULY 26

...and became man...

REFLECTION. So intense was the hatred toward Jesus that His enemies deliberately spied on him to accumulate evidence that He blasphemed God by working on the Sabbath.

Their evil intentions did not deter Him. Jesus cured the man with a withered hand on a Sabbath right before their eyes.

PRAYER. *Jesus, let not others keep me from doing good.*

HEN you choose to see the good in others, you end up finding the good in yourself. —John Spence

JULY 27

...and became man...

REFLECTION. Jesus healed a crippled woman (Lk 13:11-17), a man with dropsy (Lk 14:1-6) and a blind man (Jn 9) on a Sabbath.

He would not let someone suffer even for a day. While ordinary people recognized His goodness and rejoiced (Lk 13:17), the Pharisees became increasingly hostile.

PRAYER. *Jesus, help me see the good in others.*

EING ignorant is not so much a shame, as being unwilling to learn. —Benjamin Franklin

JULY 28

...and became man...

REFLECTION. In Jesus' day, religion was the business of the professionally trained teachers.

They became enraged when Jesus, a layman, a laborer, "a carpenter's son," attracted the crowds by His sound teaching (Mt 13:54-55). In their eyes, He had no right to speak to others about God. They were eager to silence Him.

PRAYER. *Lord Jesus, in Your words, I find strength and life.*

THE good news of the Gospel consists precisely in this—offering God's grace to the sinner! —Pope Benedict XVI

JULY 29

...and became man...

REFLECTION. The Pharisees would never cross the threshold of the house of a known sinner.

Yet, Jesus dined in the house of the hated tax-collector Matthew together with Matthew's friends. This infuriated the Pharisees (Mt 9: 9-13). They would not accept Jesus' message. They turned their hearts against Him.

PRAYER. *Jesus, friend of sinners, grant me God's grace to follow You.*

SELF-INTEREST makes some people blind... —Francois de La Rochefoucauld

JULY 30

...and became man...

REFLECTION. The Sadducees were unable to accept Jesus. These aristocrats, aligned with Rome, judged Him a political revolutionary bent on leading a revolt.

Since this would end their political power and prestige, they joined the Pharisees in looking to do away with Jesus. They complained to Pilate that Jesus was claiming to be a king to replace Caesar (Lk 23:1-3).

PRAYER. *Lord, keep me from being interested only in myself.*

I N TIME we hate that which we often fear.
—William Shakespeare

JULY 31

...and became man...

REFLECTION. The embittered hatred of the priests fueled the plot to kill Jesus. Jesus' teaching about the true nature of religion made them fear losing their privileged status.

The Hosannas of the crowds at Jesus' entry into Jerusalem maddened them. Jesus' cleansing the Temple enraged them. They kept looking "to arrest Jesus by deceit and put him to death" (Mk 14:1).

PRAYER. *Lord, shepherd me beyond all fears.*

C HRIST died for our sins. —1 Cor 15:3

AUG. 1

...For our sake he was crucified...

REFLECTION. The Cross was no accident of history. Three times Jesus predicted it (Mk 8:31; 9:31; 10:33).

Jesus accepted the Cross as God's way of destroying our sins with grace, our hatred with love, and our death with eternal life. Jesus, who lived His whole life for others, died that all of us might live for God.

PRAYER. *Jesus, my Crucified Redeemer, wash me of my sins.*

E MADE him who did not know sin to be sin for our sake... —2 Cor 5:21

AUG. 2

...For our sake he was crucified...

REFLECTION. Jesus was innocent and sinless. Yet, He willingly endured the Cross as an act of expiation for the sins of the entire world.

He took to Himself the punishment we merit so that we might receive the mercy we could never merit. No matter how great our sins might be, His mercy is even greater. God's mercy is His infinite love forgiving us sinners.

PRAYER. *Jesus, my Crucified Lord, Your mercy is truly greater than my greatest sin.*

HE Holy Spirit in a manner known only to God offers to every person the possibility of being associated with [the] paschal mystery. —*Gaudium et Spes*, 22

AUG. 3

...For our sake he was crucified...

REFLECTION. Jesus died for everyone. He stretched out His hands on the Cross in an eternal embrace of divine forgiveness for all.

God wills not the death of the sinner but that all be converted and saved (Ezek 33:11).

PRAYER. *By Your Cross, O Jesus, You redeem the world.*

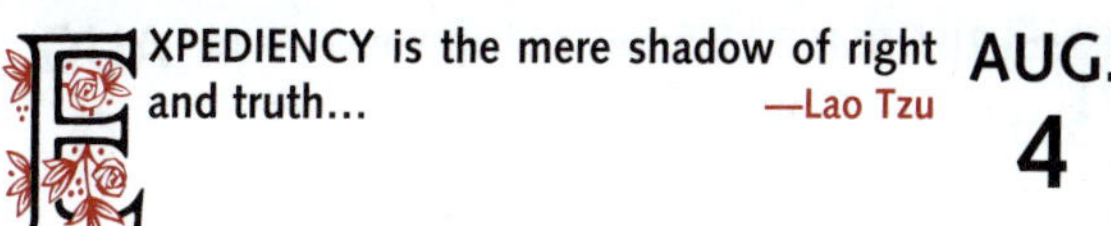

EXPEDIENCY is the mere shadow of right and truth... —Lao Tzu

AUG. 4

...For our sake he was crucified...

REFLECTION. The scribes and Pharisees' hatred of Jesus was great. Greater still was the enmity of the priests who judged Jesus a threat to their national security.

They conspired to crucify Jesus. As the high priest Caiaphas said, it was expedient "that one man die for the people rather than the whole nation be destroyed" (Jn 11:50).

PRAYER. *Jesus, help me always do what is right, no matter the personal cost.*

BETRAYAL betrays the betrayer.—Erica Jong

AUG. 5

...For our sake he was crucified...

REFLECTION. Judas cooperated with the priests to arrest Jesus. For thirty pieces of silver, the price of a slave, Judas betrayed the Master (Mt 26:14-16).

He was hoping that Jesus, once arrested, would usher in His kingdom with glory. He would not accept the humble Jesus because of his own desire for power and riches. In the end, he lost all hope and life itself.

PRAYER. *Jesus, keep me faithful to You and never let me lose hope.*

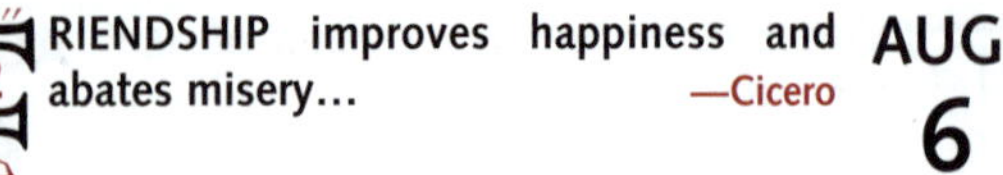

FRIENDSHIP improves happiness and abates misery... —Cicero

AUG. 6

...For our sake he was crucified...

REFLECTION. Jesus left the Last Supper singing for joy. His hour to redeem the world had come.

A few steps away in the Garden of Gethsemane, His joy darkened into deepest sorrow once He realized that His closest friends would abandon Him in His suffering. Nonetheless, trusting in the Father who never abandons us, He calmly embraced the Cross.

PRAYER. *You, O Jesus, are my most faithful and forgiving friend.*

TRUE love is inexhaustible... —Antoine de Saint-Exupery

AUG. 7

...For our sake he was crucified...

REFLECTION. In the Garden of Gethsemane, Judas betrays Jesus with a kiss. He is the only disciple to kiss Jesus.

Jesus does not draw back from Judas' treachery. He says, "My friend, do what you are here to do" (Mt 26:50). Only Jesus has true love that sees beyond our constant betrayals and offers us His friendship.

PRAYER. *Jesus, help me look beyond my sins to Your great love.*

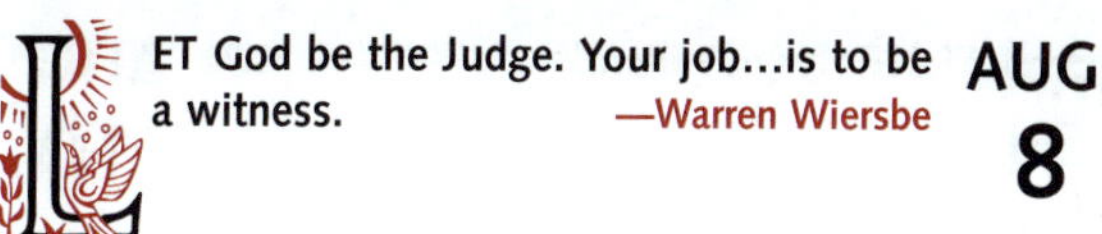

LET God be the Judge. Your job...is to be a witness. —Warren Wiersbe

AUG. 8

...For our sake he was crucified...

REFLECTION. Jesus was dragged before the Sanhedrin to be tried for blasphemy. Eager to crucify Jesus, the Jewish leaders ignored their own laws governing trials.

Under the cloak of night, they condemned Jesus to death for claiming to be God's Son. Jesus was mocked and beaten, but never wavered in witnessing to the truth.

PRAYER. *Lord Jesus, make me a faithful witness to You.*

HE WHO acts against his conscience always sins. —St. Thomas Aquinas

AUG. 9

...For our sake he was crucified...

REFLECTION. Since they could not put Jesus to death, the Jewish leaders brought Him to Pilate.

Even though Pilate found Jesus innocent of any crime, he ordered His crucifixion. Knowing he did evil, Pilate could not wash the stain of guilt from his conscience. Our conscience is an ever-present judge of our deeds.

PRAYER. *Holy Spirit, give me the grace to follow my conscience.*

FATHER, forgive them... —Lk 23:34

AUG. 10

...For our sake he was crucified...

REFLECTION. For six hours, Jesus hung dying on the Cross. It was a most painful, ignominious suffering reserved for slaves and revolutionaries.

His enemies and even passers-by taunted Him. Yet, in the greatest physical agony, Jesus remained spiritually at peace, even offering the world a divine absolution for crucifying Him. Our sins nailed Him to the Cross. His love kept Him there.

PRAYER. *Grant me, O Lord, contrition for my sins and the grace to avoid sin.*

HISTORY is a story written by the finger of God. —C. S. Lewis

AUG. 11

...under Pontius Pilate...

REFLECTION. Besides Jesus and Mary, the Creed only mentions Pilate. We know about Mary from the New Testament. But, we know about Pilate from secular history.

Thus, Pilate serves as a powerful reminder that Jesus lived and died at a specific time and place in history. Our faith springs from God's actions in history.

PRAYER. *O God, make me aware of Your Presence in my life.*

OWARDS are cruel, but the brave love mercy and delight to save. —John Gay

AUG. 12

...under Pontius Pilate...

REFLECTION. Pilate was a poor excuse for Roman justice. He knew Jesus was innocent of any crime against the state.

Yet, he had Him crucified to appease Jesus' enemies. He feared an insurrection that would unseat him from power. His self-interest blinded him to the truth and made him a coward.

PRAYER. *Holy Spirit, give me wisdom to judge rightly and courage to always do good.*

AM a king. For this was I born. —Jn18:37

AUG. 13

...under Pontius Pilate...

REFLECTION. When questioned by the pragmatic Pilate, Jesus openly claims to be king. But, He is a king so unlike Caesar.

His kingdom is founded on truth, not raw power; on love, not fear. His arm is not raised in anger to destroy His enemies, but outstretched on the wood of the Cross to embrace them with divine friendship.

PRAYER. *Lord Jesus, may Your kingdom of justice come in our day.*

JESUS is the truth which gives us peace.
—Pope Benedict XVI

AUG. 14

...under Pontius Pilate...

REFLECTION. The skeptical Pilate questions Jesus, asking Him, "What is truth?" (Jn 18:38). Then he judges the answer as irrelevant to his purposes. He wrongly equates truth with political power.

Truth can only be found in God's plan for His world, in His Eternal Word spoken in human language. Jesus standing before Pilate is Truth revealed in the flesh.

PRAYER. *Jesus, enlighten me with the knowledge of the truth.*

EVERY sin provokes its punishment.
—Amos Bronson Alcott

AUG. 15

...under Pontius Pilate...

REFLECTION. Pilate made Jesus' death legal, but he could not make it just. He stands as a reminder that the state that abhors challenges to its authority eventually ignores justice.

Pilate himself became the victim of the very state he served. Banished from office for excessive use of force on his subjects, he vanished from the annals of history.

PRAYER. *O God, "dispose my heart to follow your statutes"* (Ps 119:36).

B Y HIS bruises we have been healed.

—Isa 53:5

AUG. 16

...suffered death...

REFLECTION. Jesus' physical suffering began with a dreaded, inhumane torture inflicted by the Romans. Jesus was stripped naked and tied to a pillar.

With a whip of three or more leather tails with either bone or metal at the end, a soldier brutally scourged Jesus almost to the point of death. Cloaked in His own blood, Jesus could hardly stand or walk.

PRAYER. *My Jesus, I deeply regret how much my sins have wounded You.*

OW could I wear a crown of gold when my Lord wears a crown of thorns...?

—St. Elizabeth of Hungary

AUG. 17

...suffered death...

REFLECTION. Mocking Jesus' true royalty, the soldiers made a crown of thorns in the form of a cap.

They pressed it onto His head. So severe was the stabbing pain that any time Jesus even slightly moved, He would experience intense pain. Even a refreshing breeze against His face triggered unbearable pain.

PRAYER. *For my sins of pride, O Jesus, forgive me.*

HILE the world changes, the cross stands firm. —St. Bruno

AUG. 18

...suffered death...

REFLECTION. The soldiers laid the heavy crossbeam across Jesus' shoulders, tying it to His wrists. Abused and exhausted, Jesus willingly carried the cruel instrument of His death to the place of execution.

Three times He stumbled, falling face forward on the stone pavement. Each time, He stood up and continued His death march. He knew His Cross was our sure salvation.

PRAYER. *Jesus, I will take up my cross and follow You.*

NYONE who wishes to follow me must...take up his cross daily... —Lk 9:23

AUG. 19

...suffered death...

REFLECTION. Brutally scourged and purpled in blood, Jesus could barely carry the Cross to Calvary. The soldiers seized Simon of Cyrene to carry it for Him.

Jesus goes first. Simon follows after (Lk 23:26). This is always the way of discipleship: following Jesus, no matter what the cost.

PRAYER. *Holy Spirit, strengthen my resolve to embrace the cross in my life.*

NCE you have been to the cross, you will never be the same.—Billy Graham

AUG. 20

...suffered death...

REFLECTION. Unlike others crucified, Jesus neither curses His executioners nor blasphemes God. His enemies taunt Him.

Passers-by mock Him. Yet, Jesus, even in the midst of great suffering, remains calm. So amazed is the centurion stationed at the Cross that, at the moment of Jesus' death, he cries out, "Truly this man was the Son of God" (Mk15:39).

PRAYER. *Jesus, I believe You truly are the Son of God.*

E WAS not dragged to His sufferings, but suffered more willingly than we had greedily sinned against God.
—Stephen Charnock

AUG. 21

...suffered death...

REFLECTION. Jesus, the Son of God, took to Himself our human nature with its limitations and mortality.

He fully entered our human condition, suffering the excruciating agony of dying on the Cross so that He might sanctify every aspect of our lives, even suffering and death itself.

PRAYER. *By Your suffering and death, O Jesus, guard and protect me from sin.*

EATH is more than falling blindly into the arms of God.

—St. Maria Maravillas de Jesus

AUG. 22

...suffered death...

REFLECTION. Our experience of death is the result of sin. The body and soul are separated.

The body decays. But the soul, created by God and the subject of our consciousness, of our thinking and loving, survives the physical death of the body. At Jesus' death, His body was entombed, but His soul returned to God.

PRAYER. *By Your death, Jesus, deliver me from eternal death.*

HRIST suffered for our sins once for all, the righteous for the unrighteous...to bring you to God.

—1 Pet 3:18

AUG. 23

...suffered death...

REFLECTION. Death is the penalty for sin (Gen 2:17). In the Mosaic covenant, priests sacrificed animals, substituting them for punishment deserved by the people.

Thus, they prefigured Jesus' death. On the Cross, Jesus substituted Himself as the perfect sacrifice for us sinners, the guiltless for the guilty, and thus effected our reconciliation with God.

PRAYER. *Lamb of God, take away my sins.*

ESUS died for our sins, in accordance with the Scriptures... —1 Cor 15:3

AUG. 24

...suffered death...

REFLECTION. God cannot die. But Jesus did. Jesus is fully God and fully man. As man, He dies on the Cross.

As God, He destroys death itself. Jesus' death is not simply the result of man's injustice. The Scriptures speak of Jesus' death as part of God's eternal plan for our salvation. The road from Bethlehem leads to Golgotha.

PRAYER. *O God, You willed Jesus' death that I might live and praise You forever.*

ESUS was born to be able to die and in this way to free us from the slavery of death. —Pope Benedict XVI

AUG. 25

...suffered death...

REFLECTION. The certainty of death hangs like a heavy pall over every human life.

But, on entering the grave, Jesus trampled death beneath His feet. He lifted the veil and made death not the end of life, but the door to eternal life with God.

PRAYER. *Accompany me, O Jesus, in my living and my dying.*

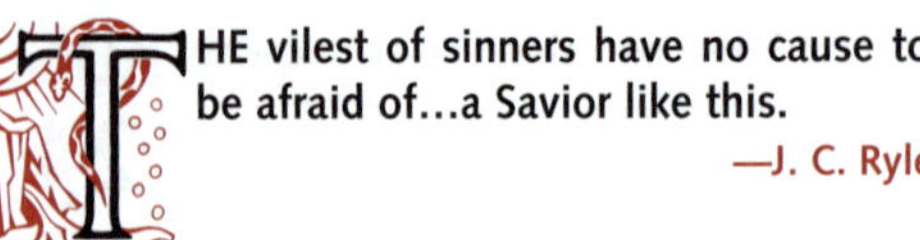

THE vilest of sinners have no cause to be afraid of...a Savior like this.

—J. C. Ryle

AUG. 26

...suffered death...

REFLECTION. Jesus' death is the supreme expression of love. Sinners watched as the Just One was unjustly murdered.

All the while, Jesus, with His heart focused on the Father's unconditional love, never stopped loving even till His dying breath. With the strength of His love, He destroyed the power of evil in the world and in us.

PRAYER. *In You, I take refuge, O Lord, from all those who would harm me.*

WHOEVER looks with faith...on the Cross, finds...the power of eternal life.

—Pope St. John Paul II

AUG. 27

...suffered death...

REFLECTION. In the Exodus events, the Hebrews sinned and were bitten by poisonous snakes.

By looking up in faith at the bronze serpent Moses placed on a pole, they were healed and lived. By faith in Jesus lifted up on the Cross, we are healed of the venom of sin and have eternal life.

PRAYER. *Heal me, O merciful Jesus, from the poison of sin.*

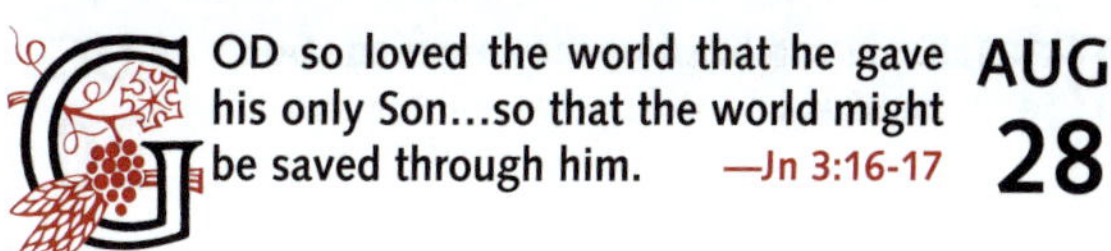

GOD so loved the world that he gave his only Son...so that the world might be saved through him. —Jn 3:16-17

AUG. 28

...suffered death...

REFLECTION. God loves us not simply because Jesus died for us. Rather, Jesus died for us because God loves us.

God sent His Son into the world to save it. In allowing Jesus to endure the Cross, the Father revealed the depth of His love for us sinners.

PRAYER. *Father, You did not spare Your Son for love of a sinner like me.*

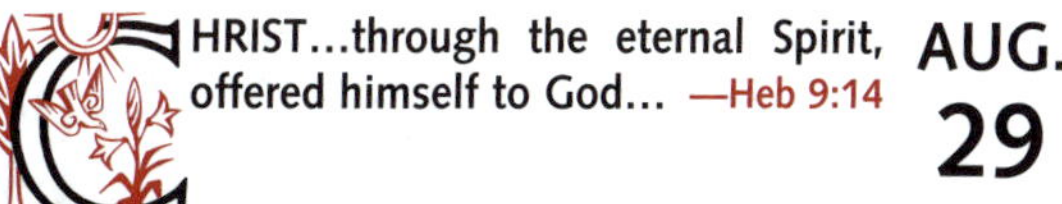

...CHRIST...through the eternal Spirit, offered himself to God... —Heb 9:14

AUG. 29

...suffered death...

REFLECTION. The Holy Spirit filled Jesus with holiness at His conception. At His Baptism, the Holy Spirt empowered Jesus for His entire ministry, even His death on the Cross.

On Golgotha, He strengthened Jesus to remain united with the Father and drain the cup of suffering to the dregs. Jesus who died as a man saved us by the power of the Holy Spirit.

PRAYER. *Holy Spirit, come and unite me to Christ Crucified.*

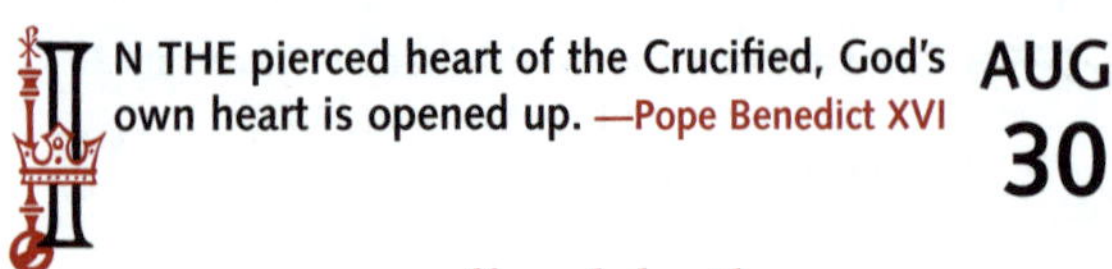

IN THE pierced heart of the Crucified, God's own heart is opened up. —Pope Benedict XVI

AUG. 30

...suffered death...

REFLECTION. To ensure He was dead, a Roman soldier thrust his spear through Jesus' side straight through His heart so wounded by our sins. His pierced heart poured out His complete love for us even to death.

There is no greater love. Through His open heart, we reach our God who is Love.

PRAYER. *Sacred Heart of Jesus, lead me to the almighty and ever-loving Father.*

THE true Holy of Holies, His Sacred Heart...opened to the guilty access to God. —Venerable Fulton Sheen

AUG. 31

...suffered death...

REFLECTION. At the moment Christ died, the heavy sixty-foot high by thirty-foot wide veil closing off the Holy of Holies to everyone except the High Priest on the Day of Atonement was torn from top to bottom.

Christ's death has opened for us access to God at every moment of our lives.

PRAYER. *Through You, Jesus, I confidently approach the throne of mercy.*

UR Lord Jesus Christ was crucified on Golgotha, nowhere else than where Adam's body lay buried.

—St. Epiphanius of Salamis

SEPT. 1

...suffered death...

REFLECTION. A tradition says that Adam was buried beneath the rock of Golgotha; and, at Christ's death, when an earthquake split the rock, Christ's blood dripped down onto Adam's bones, thus redeeming the first man.

Christ's death affects all people, past, present and future.

PRAYER. *Through Your Precious Blood, O Lord, all the descendants of Adam have hope of redemption.*

E DESCENDED, indeed, into Hades alone, but He arose accompanied by a multitude.

—St. Ignatius of Antioch

SEPT. 2

...suffered death...

REFLECTION. Matthew is the only evangelist who tells us that the earthquake at Jesus' death ripped open the tombs of many saints who had died and they arose from their graves (Mt 27:51-53).

The evangelist wants to assure us of the saving power of Christ's death even for the dead.

PRAYER. *Lord Jesus, keep me united with You in life and in death.*

JESUS was buried in a borrowed tomb because He was planning on returning it to its rightful owner after a short weekend.

—Craig D. Lounsbrough

SEPT. 3

...was buried...

REFLECTION. Nicodemus and Joseph of Arimathea, secret disciples of Jesus, anointed Jesus' body with spices and myrrh enough to embalm one hundred bodies.

They buried Him in a tomb belonging to Joseph of Arimathea. All the disciples believed this was the end.

PRAYER. *Lord Jesus, enliven my hope even in the darkest moments.*

JESUS endured... even the terror of the grave, so that he could save his people from this forever.

—H. N. Ridderbos

SEPT. 4

...was buried...

REFLECTION. Unlike others who were crucified and were left on the cross to be devoured by the birds and beasts, Jesus was buried by His friends.

He willingly descended to the lowest point of our human condition because of Adam's curse.

PRAYER. *By Your three days in the tomb, Jesus, You have made the grave the gateway to heaven.*

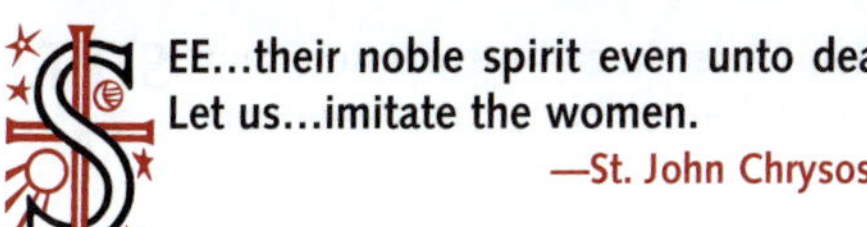

SEE...their noble spirit even unto death? Let us...imitate the women.

—St. John Chrysostom

SEPT. 5

...was buried...

REFLECTION. Mary Magdalene and Mary, the mother of Joses, sat opposite the tomb as Jesus was quickly buried.

They intended to complete the hasty embalmment once the Sabbath was over. Sitting is the position of mourning. Their tears are sacraments of their great love for Jesus.

PRAYER. *Lord Jesus, inflame my heart with a burning love for You that nothing in life or death can extinguish.*

YESTERDAY I was buried with Him; today I rise with Him.

—St. Gregory the Theologian

SEPT. 6

...was buried...

REFLECTION. Paul quotes an early Christian creed, dated a few years after Jesus, that says, "he was buried...in accordance with the Scriptures" (1 Cor 15:3-5).

The Old Testament had already prophesied Jesus' burial. Like Jonah's three days in the belly of the great fish (Jon 2:1), Jesus was three days in the tomb.

PRAYER. *Jesus, abandon me not in the darkness of the grave.*

N A garden Christ began his passion, and from a garden he would rise, and begin his exaltation. —Matthew Henry

SEPT. 7

...was buried...

REFLECTION. Death entered the world in a garden when Adam and Eve disobeyed God and sinned. Death lost its sting in another garden when Jesus was buried in a new tomb in a garden close to Golgotha (Jn 19:41).

Jesus entered that garden tomb to disarm death of its power.

PRAYER. *By Your burial, Jesus, You offer us hope of life beyond the grave.*

EVER had a crucified man had the honor of being guarded by a squad of soldiers. —E. Le Camus

SEPT. 8

...was buried...

REFLECTION. Fearing that the disciples would steal Jesus' body and proclaim the Resurrection, Jesus' enemies had Pilate seal the tomb with a stone weighing two tons.

They even had him station a guard of Roman soldiers to keep watch day and night. But no earthly power could prevent Jesus' Resurrection.

PRAYER. *Savior God, You bore fully the wages of our sins.*

E WAS not made prisoner by the powers of darkness, it is He Who exerted power amongst them. —St. Ambrose

SEPT. 9

...was buried...

REFLECTION. The Apostles' Creed says that, after Jesus was buried, "he descended into hell." This is not the hell of the damned, but the abode of the dead.

Thus, the Creed affirms that Jesus' death redeems both the living and the dead. Death cannot separate us from God.

PRAYER. *By Your death, Jesus, You save people of every time and place.*

ITHOUT the resurrection, there is no Christianity. —Gary Habermas

SEPT. 10

...and rose again...

REFLECTION. Our Christian faith is founded on the fact that the Crucified Jesus rose bodily from the dead.

Saint Paul affirms that, "if Christ has not been raised, your faith is without any foundation" (1 Cor 15:17). No founder of any other religion has been raised from the dead. Jesus' Resurrection sets Him apart as *the* bearer of God's revelation and truth.

PRAYER. *Risen Lord, in You I place my faith.*

HE hope of the resurrection is...the hope of a seismic shift...of a world-historical change. —J. Leavitt Pearl

SEPT. 11

...and rose again...

REFLECTION. After the Sabbath when the women were on the way to finish the burial rites for Jesus, "there was a violent earthquake..." (Mt 28:2).

The earth trembled as Jesus rose from the dead, trampling underfoot the oppressive powers of the world's injustice and leaving behind an empty tomb.

PRAYER. *Risen Jesus, You are the justice of God and hope for the downtrodden.*

AILURE is a school in which the truth always grows strong.

—Henry Ward Beecher

SEPT. 12

...and rose again...

REFLECTION. Mary Magdalene, Mary, the mother of James, and Salome discovered Jesus' tomb empty. An angel at the tomb told them of Jesus' Resurrection.

They were so shocked that "they fled, overcome with trembling..." (Mk 16:8). At first, they failed to tell the others, but eventually, regaining their composure, they proclaimed the Resurrection.

PRAYER. *Risen Lord, remove my fear of sharing You with others.*

HE WHO loves understands. —Kabir

SEPT. 13

...and rose again...

REFLECTION. On hearing Mary Magdalene's report of the empty tomb, Peter and John ran to see what had happened. Peter, as befitting his role as leader, first entered the empty tomb and saw the burial clothes neatly arranged.

When John then entered the tomb, "he saw and believed" (Jn 20:8). John's deep love of Jesus opened his eyes to the Resurrection even before he saw the Risen Lord.

PRAYER. *Risen Lord, grant me a believing heart.*

YOU have...the task of seeking new ways to announce Christ.

—Pope Benedict XVI

SEPT. 14

...and rose again...

REFLECTION. When Peter and John left the empty tomb, Mary Magdalene remained. Love kept her there.

Suddenly Jesus appeared to her, filling her heart with joy. He sent her to announce His Resurrection to the apostles. Like Mary Magdalene, "the apostle to the apostles," we are called to proclaim that Jesus lives.

PRAYER. *Risen Lord, make my life a faithful witness to Your presence among us.*

"DO NOT touch me..." means do not come to me if you do not acknowledge that I am God. —St. Augustine

SEPT. 15

...and rose again...

REFLECTION. When Jesus appeared to Mary Magdalene, she clung to Him with great joy.

She addressed Him as the "Teacher" she knew before His death. But Jesus told her not to cling to Him (Jn 20:17). Now, as Risen Lord and God, He will always be with His disciples.

PRAYER. *Risen Jesus, You are my Lord and God.*

WHERE Jesus is welcomed as guest, He becomes host.

—Alexander Maclaren

SEPT. 16

...and rose again...

REFLECTION. Two disciples, saddened and downcast, left Jerusalem on Easter morning with no knowledge of the Resurrection.

As they traveled, Jesus joined them, explaining the Scriptures and setting their hearts on fire. At their invitation, He sat at table with them in Emmaus. He took bread, blessed and broke it. Immediately, with the gift of the Eucharist, they recognized Him.

PRAYER. *Lord Jesus, accompany me on my life's journey.*

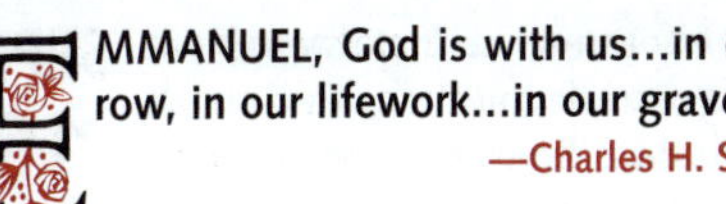

EMMANUEL, God is with us...in our sorrow, in our lifework...in our grave...
—Charles H. Spurgeon

SEPT. 17

...and rose again...

REFLECTION. On Easter evening, the Risen Lord appeared to the disciples locked behind closed doors (Jn 20:19-23; Lk 24:36-49).

Neither closed doors nor fear can block the Risen Lord from being with His disciples. As then, so now. He comes to bring us the peace of knowing that He is with us.

PRAYER. *Risen Lord, I believe and rejoice that You are always with me.*

REST assured, flesh and blood, through Christ you have gained your place in heaven...
—Tertullian

SEPT. 18

...and rose again...

REFLECTION. When the Risen Lord appeared on Easter evening to the disciples, "they thought that they were seeing a ghost" (Lk 24:37).

He showed them His wounds and then ate a piece of fish (Lk 24:42-43). He was the same Jesus they had known before His death, now raised up bodily in glory.

PRAYER. *By Your Resurrection, O Lord, You make holy our very bodies.*

IS clemency acted...so that through the doubting disciple touching the wounds in his Master's body, our own wounds of incredulity might be healed.

—Pope St. Gregory the Great

SEPT. 19

...and rose again...

REFLECTION. Thomas, absent when the Risen Lord first appeared to the disciples on Easter night, was with them when Jesus appeared a week later.

To convince doubting Thomas of the Resurrection, Jesus gently invites him to touch His wounds. Thomas sees and believes.

PRAYER. *Jesus, without seeing, I believe You are risen and active in my life.*

E CHOOSES to make Himself known... amidst the dusty commonplaces of daily life. **—Alexander Maclaren**

SEPT. 20

...and rose again...

REFLECTION. The apostles returned to Galilee where the Risen Jesus told them He would meet with them again.

Jesus appeared to them after they had an unsuccessful night of fishing. From the seashore, He told them where to fish and they hauled in an enormous catch. The Risen Lord helps us in all our needs.

PRAYER. *Lord Jesus, in Your hands I place all the deepest desires of my heart.*

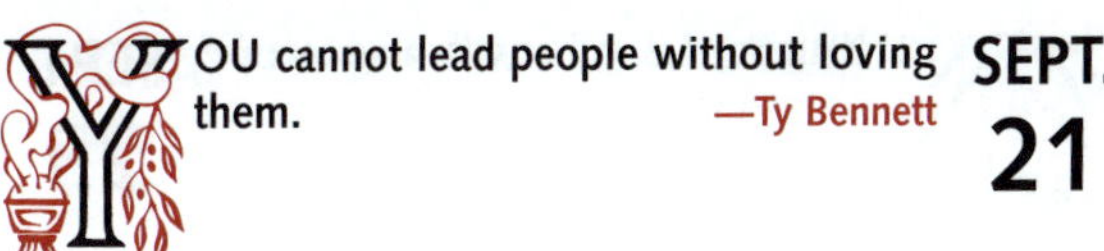

YOU cannot lead people without loving them. —Ty Bennett

SEPT. 21

...and rose again...

REFLECTION. At the Sea of Tiberias, the Risen Jesus asks Peter three times if he loves Him. Three times Peter professes his love, reversing his three denials of Jesus.

After each profession of love, Jesus commissions Peter to feed His sheep. Thus, the role of Peter and his successors of shepherding the Church must always spring from their love of Jesus.

PRAYER. *Risen Jesus, keep Your priests united in love of You and those they serve.*

THIS summons...to Peter by Christ after his resurrection...'Come follow me'... is a summons to service and a summons to die... —Pope St. John Paul II

SEPT. 22

...and rose again...

REFLECTION. After commissioning Peter to shepherd the Church, Jesus says, "Follow me" (Jn 21:19).

No one can lead without first learning to follow. Whatever our particular role in the Church is, like Peter, we are called to walk in the footsteps of Christ, even to the Cross.

PRAYER. *Risen Lord, may I always be Your faithful follower.*

ON THE third day, he will raise us up.
—Hos 6:2

SEPT. 23

...on the third day in accordance with the Scriptures...

REFLECTION. On the third day, Isaac is saved from being sacrificed on Mt. Moriah, Moses encounters God on Mt. Sinai, the Israelites enter the Promised Land, and Jonah escapes the belly of the great fish.

In raising Jesus from the dead on the third day, God accomplishes our salvation as foreshadowed in Scripture.

PRAYER. *Risen Lord, give me a share in Your third day when my life on earth is ended.*

OUR Lord Jesus Christ ascended into heaven; let our hearts ascend with Him.
—St. Augustine

SEPT. 24

...He ascended into heaven...

REFLECTION. After appearing for forty days to His disciples, the Risen Lord ascended to heaven. His Ascension is "the irreversible entry of his humanity into divine glory..." (*Catechism of the Catholic Church*, 659).

The Ascension brings to completion our salvation begun with the Incarnation. We are destined for the glory of heaven.

PRAYER. *Lord Jesus, keep my eyes fixed on You.*

IS ascension...amidst the acclamations of angels...is the sure proof that the work is complete.

—Charles H. Spurgeon

SEPT. 25

...He ascended into heaven...

REFLECTION. When Jesus entered Jerusalem on Palm Sunday, the crowds hailed Him as the Messiah King.

Wearing the crown of thorns, He ascended the Cross and died for us. Ascending to heaven, He triumphantly enters the heavenly Jerusalem and is crowned with glory, inaugurating His everlasting reign over creation.

PRAYER. *To You, O Christ, be glory and praise and honor forever.*

HE body...is capable of making visible what is invisible: the spiritual and the divine.

—Pope St. John Paul II

SEPT. 26

...He ascended into heaven...

REFLECTION. Ascending into heaven, Jesus brings our humanity, our flesh and blood, into the very mystery of God Himself.

This is good news for us. Christ's Ascension shows us how much God values and loves our body which He created to image His glory. Our bodies, indeed, are sacred.

PRAYER. *Lord Jesus, help us respect and care for the gift of our bodies.*

E IS now in the lordship of God, present in every space and time, close to each one of us. —Pope Francis

SEPT. 27

...He ascended into heaven...

REFLECTION. When Jesus ascended to heaven, a cloud took Him from the sight of the disciples (Acts 1:9).

Nevertheless, they were "filled with great joy" (Lk 24:52). They realized that Jesus, no longer bound by the limits of this world, is with us wherever we are.

PRAYER. *Jesus, fill me with the joy of Your presence so that others may come to know You as Lord.*

OW insignificant earth seems to me when I consider Heaven.

—St. Ignatius of Loyola

SEPT. 28

...He ascended into heaven...

REFLECTION. Jesus promised that He was going to heaven to prepare a place for us (Jn 14:1-3).

We have in this world no lasting home. Our true home is with Jesus in heaven. Where He is, there we are meant to be. We are pilgrims on our way to glory.

PRAYER. *Lord Jesus, keep my eyes and heart set on being with You in heaven.*

E HAVE an Advocate with the Father, Jesus Christ...himself the sacrifice of our sins. —1 Jn 2:1-2

SEPT. 29

...He ascended into heaven...

REFLECTION. Because Jesus who has ascended to heaven stands before the Father as our advocate, we never despair because of our sinfulness.

The Father sees in Jesus the perfect atonement for our sins and bestows on us through Jesus the graces we need to live holy lives pleasing to God.

PRAYER. *Almighty Father, look on Your Beloved Son and grant me mercy.*

HO will condemn? Christ Jesus, who...intercedes for us?... —Rom 8:34

SEPT. 30

...He ascended into heaven...

REFLECTION. Ascended to heaven, Jesus intercedes for us before the Father when we approach God through Him (Heb 7:25).

In all our struggles and trials, Jesus prays for us and with us that we have the strength to do what is right and just for our eternal salvation. Thus, our prayers for divine assistance do not go unheard.

PRAYER. *Lord Jesus, I place all my prayers and petitions in Your hands.*

HRIST Jesus [is] our Lord, and God, and Savior, and King, according to the will of the invisible Father.

—St. Irenaeus

OCT. 1

...seated at the right hand of the Father...

REFLECTION. A king placing someone on his right gave him the highest honor, conferring on him equal authority and dignity.

The image of Jesus seated at the right hand of the Father expresses His equality with the Father. He is truly God with divine authority and majesty.

PRAYER. *Lord Jesus, I adore You enthroned in glory.*

E IS the true King...seated in heaven... with every adversary at his feet, until...the last enemy, death, be defeated by him once and for all.

—Pope Benedict XVI

OCT. 2

...seated at the right hand of the Father...

REFLECTION. Enthroned at the Father's right hand, Jesus rules over all creation.

He guides the world so that people of every race and nation come to experience justice, peace, and life eternal.

PRAYER. *To You, Jesus, King of all creation, I offer the obedience of my whole life.*

HEY went forth to proclaim the gospel, while the Lord worked with them...

—Mk 16:20

OCT. 3

...seated at the right hand of the Father...

REFLECTION. At the Last Supper, Jesus promised not to leave us orphans (Jn 14:18).

Exalted to God's right hand, He helps us bring the gospel in word and deed to others. He inspires us with His grace and works in and through us for the redemption of the world.

PRAYER. *Lord Jesus, help me always cooperate with You in Your redemptive work.*

E NEED no wings to go in search of Him, but have only to look upon Him present within us.

—St. Teresa of Avila

OCT. 4

...seated at the right hand of the Father...

REFLECTION. Before ascending to heaven, Jesus promised to be with us "always, to the end of the world" (Mt 28:20).

Now from the right hand of the Father, He strengthens us in our trials and assures us of hope in our struggles.

PRAYER. *Lord Jesus, You are my comfort and joy. With You beside me, I have nothing to fear.*

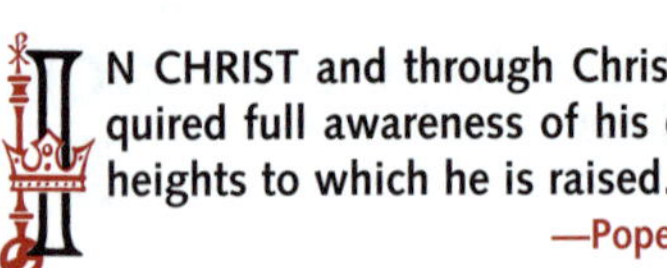
N CHRIST and through Christ man has acquired full awareness of his dignity, of the heights to which he is raised...

—Pope St. John Paul II

OCT. 5

...seated at the right hand of the Father...

REFLECTION. When Adam sinned, humanity, made in the image and likeness of God, lost its royal dignity.

When Jesus ascended to heaven and is seated at the Father's right hand, humanity regained its royal dignity.

PRAYER. *Lord Jesus, help me live as worthy of the dignity You give me.*

E PREACH not one advent only of Christ, but a second also, far more glorious than the former.

—St. Cyril of Jerusalem

OCT. 6

...He will come again in glory...

REFLECTION. Twenty-one times Jesus spoke of His second coming. He first came to earth in humility, suffering death for our redemption.

Victorious over sin and death, He will come again to bring us with Him to share the glory of heaven.

PRAYER. *Lord Jesus, stir up in me an eager longing for Your return.*

THE man of sin...must first be revealed before the Lord comes, who...exalts himself...as being God. —Tertullian

OCT. 7

...He will come again in glory...

REFLECTION. Jesus predicted that there would be a final trial before He returns again (Mt 24: 4-14). False prophets will turn people from the truth of the gospel, causing them to apostatize.

This final rebellion in which man claims to be God (2 Thes 2:1-10) will test the faithful.

PRAYER. *Lord Jesus, keep me faithful to the truth and to the Church You have founded.*

MANY antichrists have already come. Thus, we know that it is the final hour. —1 Jn 2:18

OCT. 8

...He will come again in glory...

REFLECTION. Before Christ returns, the Antichrist will appear. The Antichrist will be either one individual or many individuals preaching a secular messianism.

The Antichrist will deceive others into believing that this world is all that there is and that we ourselves can achieve a perfect society on earth without God.

PRAYER. *Lord Jesus Christ, You alone are my Savior today, tomorrow, forever.*

ET us remain firm in the confession of our hope without wavering, for he who promised is trustworthy. —Heb 10:23

OCT. 9

...He will come again in glory...

REFLECTION. Before Jesus returns, the battle of Armageddon, the final, decisive battle between good and evil, will take place.

In this climactic confrontation, the forces of Satan will conspire together against God. But Christ's victory is assured (Rev 19:15). Therefore, we can be courageous when we face evil.

PRAYER. *Deliver me, O Lord, from all evil wherever and whenever it comes.*

OD will not allow you to be tried beyond your strength... —1 Cor 10:13

OCT. 10

...He will come again in glory...

REFLECTION. In the *Our Father*, when we pray, "lead us not into temptation" (Mt 6:13), we ask God to keep us from falling into sin.

However, with this petition, we pray to be spared the final chaos and corruption of the end time. We implore God to preserve us from the full force of evil.

PRAYER. *Father, keep me faithful under Your protection until the very end.*

HE Lord has given us the first fruits of the taste of what is yet to be.

—St. Ephrem

OCT. 11

...He will come again in glory...

REFLECTION. Christ's Second Coming will bring to completion all God's promises. It will be the final, definitive defeat of evil and the full revelation of God's goodness.

Creation itself will not be destroyed but transformed. We who live united with Christ already enjoy the pledge of what is to come.

PRAYER. *You, Lord, are the world's hope. In You, all things will be made new.*

EEP alert, because you do not know when the time will come. —Mk 13:33

OCT. 12

...He will come again in glory...

REFLECTION. No one knows the exact day of Jesus' return. It will catch many by surprise.

Like the wise virgins in the Parable of the Ten Virgins who kept their lamps ready to welcome the bridegroom (Mt 25:1-13), we need to be prepared by a good life to welcome the Lord when He comes.

PRAYER. *Lord Jesus, help me live always in Your grace.*

HE Coming of the Prince of Peace is a promise that everything that is damaged by sin will be restored.

—Paul Tripp

OCT. 13

...He will come again in glory...

REFLECTION. The New Testament uses the Greek word *parousia* seventeen times for Jesus' return.

This word originally described the arrival of a king coming to show his goodness to his people. At Jesus' return, we will fully understand how much He loves and cares for us.

PRAYER. *With joy, O Jesus, I await Your return and the restoration of all good.*

VERY Eucharist is Parousia, the Lord's coming. **—Pope Benedict XVI**

OCT. 14

...He will come again in glory...

REFLECTION. The *Didache* (c. 70 A.D.) contains the most ancient Eucharistic prayer that we have. This Eucharistic prayer ends with the Aramaic word *Maranatha* (Come, Lord!).

For in every Eucharist, the Risen Glorified Christ who will come at the end of time already comes. He is truly present to us, preparing us to meet Him at His Second Coming in glory.

PRAYER. *Come, Lord Jesus!*

THE Father judges no one, for he has entrusted all judgment to the Son.

—Jn 5:22

OCT. 15

...to judge the living and the dead...

REFLECTION. By His Cross and Resurrection, Jesus has redeemed us, rescuing us from eternal damnation and offering us the grace to be saved. He who is our Savior will also be our Judge when He returns.

He will judge our lives by our acceptance or refusal of His grace.

PRAYER. *Savior of the world, be for me a merciful Judge.*

NO SOONER shall we have breathed our last sigh than our soul...will be presented before the tribunal of God.

—St. John Vianney

OCT. 16

...to judge the living and the dead...

REFLECTION. Immediately at death, we will stand "before the judgment seat of Christ" (2 Cor 5:10).

In that instant, we will see our entire life either as a response or rejection of Christ's love for us and learn from His lips our eternal fate.

PRAYER. *Lord Jesus, grant me a happy death and eternal union with You.*

LREADY before they take up their bodies...they will be...in the heavenly kingdom...joined to the company of the holy angels.

—Benedictus Deus

OCT. 17

...to judge the living and the dead...

REFLECTION. At the moment of death, Jesus will judge those who have died in perfect charity worthy to enter heaven immediately.

Even before the end of the world, they will enjoy being with God whom they have so well served while on earth.

PRAYER. *Lord Jesus, please grant me perfect charity and a place with You in heaven.*

HE purifying fires draw them ever upward and closer to God.

—St. Catherine of Genoa

OCT. 18

...to judge the living and the dead...

REFLECTION. Those who die in an imperfect friendship with God, Christ judges worthy of heaven once purified of their sins.

This purification is called Purgatory. It is the fire of love, the intense desire to be with God, that burns away their imperfections and readies them to be with the all-perfect God.

PRAYER. *Lord, purify my love of You and remove from me every stain of sin.*

THE fire which both burns and saves is Christ himself, the Judge and Savior.

—Pope Benedict XVI

OCT. 19

...to judge the living and the dead...

REFLECTION. Christ's judgment of Purgatory for someone at death is an act of great mercy.

His gaze penetrates the soul with love so overwhelming that the individual is pained by his or her failures to love God. Purgatory is an experience of grace that prepares the soul for communion with God.

PRAYER. *All just Jesus, in Your mercy I place my hope.*

HELL...exists and is eternal for those who shut their hearts to his love.

—Pope Benedict XVI

OCT. 20

...to judge the living and the dead...

REFLECTION. Those who die unrepentant of their sins and in a state of mortal sin, that is, alienated from God by their own choice, cannot enter heaven.

In judging them, Christ respects their choice and allows them to remain for all eternity in that state of exclusion from God which is called "hell."

PRAYER. *My Savior Lord, guard my choices and preserve me in Your grace.*

HE last judgment shall fill sinners with terror, but will be a source of joy...to the elect. —St. Alphonsus de Liguori

OCT. 21

...to judge the living and the dead...

REFLECTION. At the end of time, Christ will judge the living and the dead.

This Last Judgment will not change but only reveal Christ's judgment on those who had already died. He will call the elect to be with Him forever and send away the damned. (Mt 25:31-46).

PRAYER. *I cry out to You O Lord, save me from final damnation.*

OTHING can so terrify us as much as Jesus Christ can reassure us. —St. John of Avila

OCT. 22

...to judge the living and the dead...

REFLECTION. At the Last Judgment, Christ will reveal how God worked throughout all of history in the lives of each person.

He will let us see how God's providence brought creation and history to achieve His purpose. He will show us how God's love ultimately prevailed over the world's evils.

PRAYER. *Lord, let me not fear Your judgment but have great trust in Your mercy.*

OF HIS kingdom there will be no end. —Lk 1:33

OCT. 23

...his kingdom will have no end...

REFLECTION. The kingdom of God was the central teaching of Jesus. He began His ministry announcing its arrival (Mk 1:15).

His mighty works proclaimed its presence (Mt 12:28). His words invited us to enter the kingdom. He instructed us to pray, "Thy kingdom come" (Mt 6:10). Enthroned on the Cross, He inaugurated His kingdom.

PRAYER. *Holy Spirit, lead me always into the kingdom of Jesus.*

BEHOLD, the kingdom of God is in your midst. —Lk 17:21

OCT. 24

...his kingdom will have no end...

REFLECTION. During His public ministry, Jesus taught that the future and final kingdom that He would fully establish at His Second Coming was already present in us.

The kingdom is simply God's sovereign rule over all. Thus, where God's will is done, there is the kingdom.

PRAYER. *Father, Lord of heaven and earth, help me always to do Your will as taught by Jesus.*

HAVE a mustard seed; and I am not afraid to use it. —Pope Benedict XVI

OCT. 25

...his kingdom will have no end...

REFLECTION. Jesus compared the kingdom not to the noble cedar but to the small, seemingly insignificant mustard seed that grows large enough to welcome the birds of the sky (Mt 13:31-32).

By this comparison, He taught us that our small, ordinary acts done in His name are actually bringing about His universal kingdom.

PRAYER. *Jesus, let all I do further Your kingdom.*

OD moves in a mysterious way, His wonders to perform. —William Cowper

OCT. 26

...his kingdom will have no end...

REFLECTION. Jesus taught that His kingdom would gradually come about like the leaven a woman puts into dough (Mt 13:33).

He wanted us to realize the hidden nature of His kingdom. In ways that we cannot see now, His kingdom is gradually growing in our world and one day will be revealed.

PRAYER. *God, our Creator and Redeemer, You are great in all Your works.*

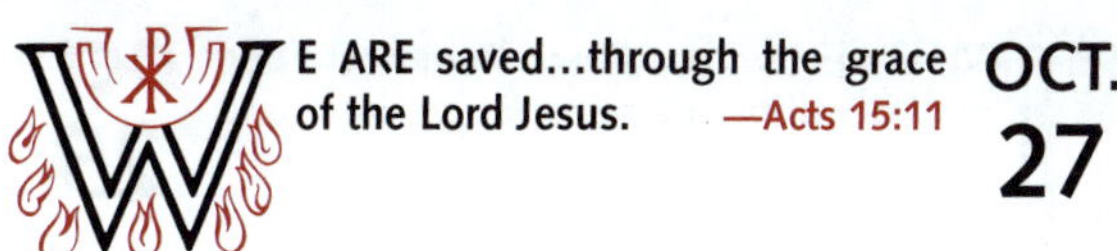

WE ARE saved...through the grace of the Lord Jesus. —Acts 15:11

OCT. 27

...his kingdom will have no end...

REFLECTION. Jesus likened the kingdom to a treasure hidden in a field that a man stumbles upon by chance. As a result, his whole life is changed for the better (Mt 13:44).

By this illustration, He taught us that belonging to the kingdom is a gift given to us by God out of His gracious mercy.

PRAYER. *Lord Jesus, I trust totally in Your plentiful and undeserved grace.*

IF THE kingdom of God is not first, it doesn't matter what's second. —Neal A. Maxwell

OCT. 28

...his kingdom will have no end...

REFLECTION. Jesus taught that the kingdom was like a pearl of great price for which a man sold all that he had to possess it (Mt 13:45).

In other words, God's kingdom should be our priority. We should be willing to make any sacrifice necessary to remain under God's sovereign rule.

PRAYER. *Lord Jesus, help me seek first God's kingdom.*

HE Lord...is slow to anger and abounding in kindness. —Ps 103:8

OCT. 29

...his kingdom will have no end...

REFLECTION. Jesus likened the kingdom to a field where the owner sowed wheat, but an enemy sowed weeds.

Only at harvest time will the wheat be separated from the weeds. By this parable, Jesus emphasized His patience with sinners giving them time to repent before their final judgment (Mt 13:24-30).

PRAYER. *Lord Jesus, help me be slow to condemn others and quick to encourage their goodness.*

AVE faith with love. This is the wedding garment. —St. Augustine

OCT. 30

...his kingdom will have no end...

REFLECTION. Jesus' kingdom is like a wedding banquet open to everyone.

Yet, whoever shows up without a wedding garment is cast "outside into the darkness, where there will be weeping and gnashing of teeth" (Mt 22:13). We are to take seriously our invitation to belong to His kingdom by living a good life.

PRAYER. *Lord Jesus, give me the faith that leads to charity toward all.*

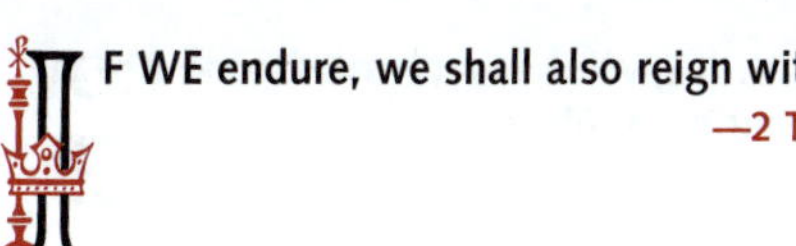

IF WE endure, we shall also reign with him. —2 Tim 2:12

OCT. 31

...his kingdom will have no end...

REFLECTION. In the end, Christ will destroy all the powers of evil and even death itself and the Father will make everything subject to Him (1 Cor 15:27).

Those who have been faithful citizens of Christ's kingdom on earth will share in His kingship in our true home in heaven. Until then, we are exiles on earth.

PRAYER. *Father, keep me faithful to Your Son.*

THIS Lord is the Spirit. —2 Cor 3:17

NOV. 1

...I believe in the Holy Spirit, the Lord...

REFLECTION. The Holy Spirit is not an impersonal force or power emanating from God. The Holy Spirit has a mind (1 Cor 2:10-11) and a will (1 Cor 12:11).

The Holy Spirit is all-knowing and all-seeing (Acts 5:3-4). The Holy Spirit is the third Person of the Blessed Trinity, one God with the Father and the Son.

PRAYER. *Holy Spirit, You truly are Lord and God.*

HE Spirit...is given...as a divine supernatural spring of life and action.

—Jonathan Edwards

NOV. 2

...I believe in the Holy Spirit, the Lord...

REFLECTION. As Lord, the Holy Spirit directed the course of Israel's history. The Spirit came upon Moses, making him Israel's greatest prophet and mediator of the old covenant.

So filled was Moses with the Holy Spirit that he was able to share the Holy Spirit with the seventy elders (Num 11:24-25).

PRAYER. *Holy Spirit, help me see and give thanks for Your presence in others.*

HE work of the Spirit is to impart life, to implant hope, to give liberty...

—Dwight L. Moody

NOV. 3

...I believe in the Holy Spirit, the Lord...

REFLECTION. The Holy Spirit brought the Chosen People to life during the Exodus events.

Symbolized by the pillar of cloud by day and fire by night, the Holy Spirit led the fugitives from Egypt, forming them as God's people (Ex 13:21-22). The Holy Spirit makes us part of God's people.

PRAYER. *Holy Spirit, keep me always united to God's people.*

TAKE Joshua, a man in whom the Spirit is found and lay your hand on him.

—Num 27:18

NOV. 4

...I believe in the Holy Spirit, the Lord...

REFLECTION. To succeed Moses and complete his work, God filled Joshua with the Holy Spirit. He gave him the boldness and courage needed to lead Israel into the Promised Land.

Joshua foreshadows Jesus, who filled with the Holy Spirit, leads us to heaven, the true Promised Land.

PRAYER. *Holy Spirit, keep alive in me the desire to always follow Jesus.*

HE WILL give you another Advocate to be with you forever, the Spirit of Truth.

—Jn 14:16

NOV. 5

...I believe in the Holy Spirit, the Lord...

REFLECTION. After Joshua's death, the Holy Spirit came upon certain individuals called "judges." He stayed with them temporarily, empowering them to save Israel from their enemies.

To us who believe in Christ and are baptized, the Father gives the Holy Spirit to stay with us and keep us from evil.

PRAYER. *Holy Spirit, save me from the wiles of Satan and all evil spirits.*

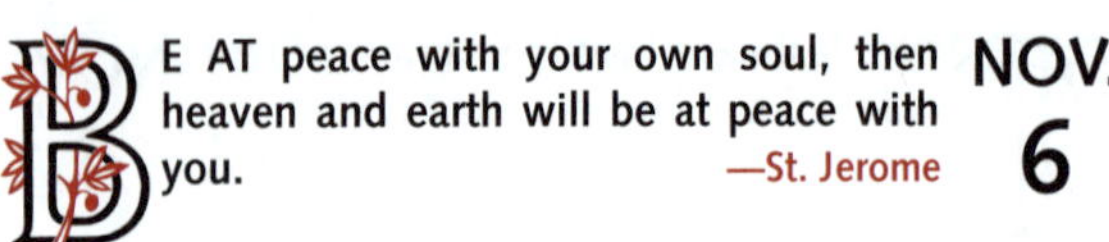

BE AT peace with your own soul, then heaven and earth will be at peace with you.
—St. Jerome

NOV. 6

...I believe in the Holy Spirit, the Lord...

REFLECTION. Othniel was Israel's first judge. "The Spirit of the Lord came upon him" (Jdg 3:10) and he conquered the king of Mesopotamia, bringing peace to Israel for nearly a half century.

Jesus, filled with the Spirit, conquered sin and death on the Cross, bringing lasting peace to the world.

PRAYER. *Lord, grant me true peace of soul.*

GOD chose those in the world who were weak to shame the strong.
—1 Cor 1:27

NOV. 7

...I believe in the Holy Spirit, the Lord...

REFLECTION. "The Holy Spirit came upon Gideon" (Jdg 6:34) and he delivered Israel from the powerful Midianites.

Gideon lacked courage and was of weak faith. Yet, the Holy Spirit used him to accomplish God's will. We should never fear letting God have His way with us.

PRAYER. *Holy Spirit, make me, weak as I am, an instrument of Your peace.*

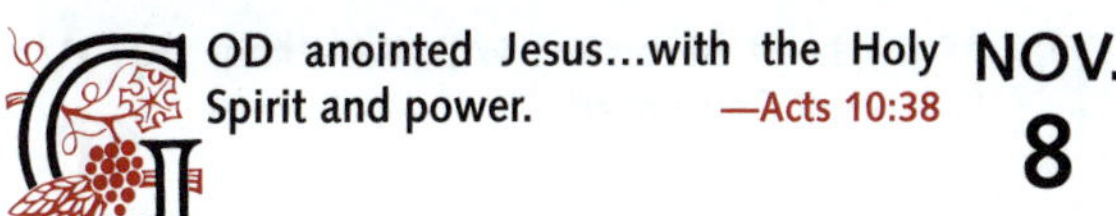

GOD anointed Jesus...with the Holy Spirit and power. —Acts 10:38

NOV. 8

...I believe in the Holy Spirit, the Lord...

REFLECTION. Samson accomplished great feats of strength. "The Spirit of the Lord rushed upon him..." (Jdg 14:6, 19; 15:14) and he tore a lion apart with his hands, slaughtered his enemies, and killed thousands with a donkey's jawbone.

The Spirit who suddenly came to Samson was always with Jesus, empowering Him to work His miracles and exorcisms.

PRAYER. *Holy Spirit, empower me always to do good to others.*

IF YOU keep my commandments...the Father will give you the Spirit... —Jn 14:15-17

NOV. 9

...I believe in the Holy Spirit, the Lord...

REFLECTION. When Samuel anointed Saul as Israel's first king, the Spirit of the Lord came upon him to guide him (1 Sam 10:10).

However, when he disobeyed God, "the Spirit of the Lord...departed from Saul" (1 Sam 16:14) and he lost his kingship. The Holy Spirit works in us when we obey God's will.

PRAYER. *Lord, by Your Holy Spirit, keep me always obedient to Your will.*

LET my heart be broken with the things that break God's heart. —Bob Pierce

NOV. 10

...I believe in the Holy Spirit, the Lord...

REFLECTION. David, Israel's greatest king, reigned for forty years. He united Israel and secured her borders.

From the day of his anointing, he was led by the Holy Spirit (1 Sam 16:13). When he sinned, he humbly prayed, "Do not take from me your Holy Spirit" (Ps 51:13); and, God forgave him.

PRAYER. *Holy Spirit, give me a contrite and humble heart.*

THE Spirit is Creator, Whom we know as the Author of the Lord's Incarnation. —St. Ambrose

NOV. 11

...I believe in the Holy Spirit, the Lord...

REFLECTION. The moment Mary consented to the angel Gabriel's message to be the Mother of the Messiah, the Holy Spirit overshadowed her. By the power of the Holy Spirit, the eternal Son of God took our human nature and became man (Lk 1:35).

The Holy Spirit works to accomplish our salvation in Christ.

PRAYER. *Holy Spirit, keep me always one with Christ.*

T HIS baptism...Jesus...received a special outpouring of the Holy Spirit...as the Spirit of reconciliation and divine goodwill.

—Pope St. John Paul II

NOV. 12

...I believe in the Holy Spirit, the Lord...

REFLECTION. The Holy Spirit whom Jesus possessed from the moment of the Incarnation came on Jesus at His baptism in the Jordan River, empowering Him for His mission as our Savior (Mt 3:16).

Everything Jesus did, He did in the power of the Holy Spirit.

PRAYER. *By the power of the Holy Spirit, save me, O Lord.*

OD does not prevent temptations... that you may in this way be made stronger. **—St. John Chrysostom**

NOV. 13

...I believe in the Holy Spirit, the Lord...

REFLECTION. After His Baptism, "Jesus was led by the Spirit into the desert...where he was tempted" (Lk 4:1-2).

God allowed the devil to tempt Jesus so that Jesus, led by the Spirit, could, by resisting the temptations, be strengthened to do God's will as Messiah. In every temptation, the Holy Spirit helps us.

PRAYER. *Holy Spirit, strengthen me to resist temptations.*

HEN you sent forth your Spirit, they were created... —Ps 104:30

NOV. 14

...the giver of life...

REFLECTION. As an eagle hovers over its nest when new life is being brought forth (Deut 32:11), the Holy Spirit hovered over the formless void and barren earth (Gen 1:2) at the first moment of creation.

The Holy Spirit brought forth the created world in all its wonder and order, giving life to all living things.

PRAYER. *Holy Spirit, Lord and Creator, order my days in righteousness.*

T IS the Spirit that gives life; the flesh can achieve nothing. —Jn 6:63

NOV. 15

...the giver of life...

REFLECTION. When God formed Adam from the dust of the earth and "breathed his breath of life" into him (Gen 2:7), the Holy Spirit made Adam a living person.

The Holy Spirit keeps us in existence. As Job confesses, "If he would take back his Spirit...all mankind would turn again to dust" (Job 34:14-15).

PRAYER. *Holy Spirit, guard and protect the life You give me.*

HE Spirit of him who raised Jesus from the dead dwells in you... —Rom 8:11

NOV. 16

...the giver of life...

REFLECTION. By the power of the Holy Spirit, the Father raised Jesus from the dead, totally transforming His human body.

Filled with the Holy Spirit, the Risen Lord has become "a life-giving spirit" (1 Cor 15:45). He imparts the Holy Spirit to all who believe, making us sharers in God's eternal life.

PRAYER. *Lord Jesus, by the gift of Your Spirit, make me a sharer in God's own life.*

ERE it not for the work of the Holy Spirit there would be no gospel, no faith, no church... —J. I. Packer

NOV. 17

...the giver of life...

REFLECTION. On Pentecost, the Holy Spirit descended on the first followers of Jesus and the Church was born, not by the work of man, but by the grace of God.

The Holy Spirit united them into a community of faith, eager to share the Gospel.

PRAYER. *Holy Spirit, keep me always united to the Church.*

OUR body is the temple of the Holy Spirit within you... —1 Cor 6:19

NOV. 18

...the giver of life...

REFLECTION. At Baptism, the Holy Spirit comes to us and we are changed.

He gives us a share in the life of the Trinity and we are "born again of water and the Spirit" (Jn 3:5) as children of God (Gal 4:6). The Holy Spirit indwells in us, sanctifying, encouraging, and sustaining us in all our trials.

PRAYER. *Come Holy Spirit, and never depart from me.*

HE Holy Spirit is the soul of the Church. —Pope Francis

NOV. 19

...the giver of life...

REFLECTION. The Holy Spirit continually breathes new life into the Church.

The Spirit impels the Church to continue the mission of Jesus by proclaiming the Gospel and drawing all people into the mystery of communion with the Most Holy Trinity. The Holy Spirit inspires each one of us to be a missionary disciple.

PRAYER. *Holy Spirit, stir up in me the desire to share Christ with others.*

LET yourselves be led by the Holy Spirit with freedom... —Pope Francis

NOV. 20

...the Holy Spirit, the Lord...

REFLECTION. The Greek text of Isaiah 11:1-3 lists seven gifts which the Holy Spirit bestows on the Messiah.

These gifts which Jesus fully possessed we receive at Baptism as a permanent endowment strengthened within us by Confirmation. They help us to heed the promptings of the Holy Spirit in our following of Jesus.

PRAYER. *Holy Spirit, help me always use the gifts You give me.*

WISDOM is...the grace of being able to see everything with the eyes of God. —Pope Francis

NOV. 21

...the Holy Spirit, the Lord...

REFLECTION. Among the seven gifts of the Holy Spirit, wisdom holds the place of primacy.

It enables us to see and judge everything according to divine truth. Gifted with wisdom, we see beyond the particulars of life to the plan of God who orders all things for our eternal salvation.

PRAYER. *Holy Spirit, help me see all things as You see them.*

NO ONE comprehends what pertains to God, except the Spirit of God.

—1 Cor 2:11

NOV. 22

...the Holy Spirit, the Lord...

REFLECTION. Our intellect is limited. By reason alone, we cannot fully comprehend the mysteries of our faith.

Therefore, the Holy Spirit gives us the gift of understanding, enabling us to grasp more easily the truths revealed by God. The Holy Spirit also helps us see how truths known by reason are related to our supernatural destiny.

PRAYER. *Holy Spirit, enlighten my use of knowledge and reason.*

GOD brought things into being in order that his goodness might be communicated to creatures...

—St. Thomas Aquinas

NOV. 23

...the Holy Spirit, the Lord...

REFLECTION. All God created reflects His Truth and His Beauty. By the Holy Spirit's gift of knowledge, we can contemplate creation and recognize God's goodness.

We see all things as dependent on God and do not give to created things more value than they rightly deserve.

PRAYER. *Holy Spirit, lead me to praise God for the goodness of creation.*

OUNSEL...is the gift through which the Holy Spirit enables our conscience to make a concrete choice...according to the logic of Jesus and his Gospel.

—Pope Francis

NOV. 24

...the Holy Spirit, the Lord...

REFLECTION. The gift of counsel helps us discern between good acts that should be done and sinful acts that should be avoided.

Furthermore, it stirs up within us an attraction to what is good and a repugnance to what is evil.

PRAYER. *Holy Spirit, help me form a right conscience so that I may always do good and avoid evil.*

HEN one is convinced that his cause is just, he will fear nothing.

—St. John Bosco

NOV. 25

...the Holy Spirit, the Lord...

REFLECTION. With the gift of fortitude, the Holy Spirit helps us to do what is right in difficult moments. Fortitude conquers all complacency, apathy, and fear.

It puts us on the path to action in the face of danger, making us willing to do what is right, even at great self-sacrifice.

PRAYER. *Lord, give me the courage to do Your will.*

TRUE piety hath in it nothing weak, nothing sad, nothing constrained. It enlarges the heart... —Francois Fenelon

NOV. 26

...the Holy Spirit, the Lord...

REFLECTION. By the gift of piety, the Holy Spirit moves us to worship God as our loving Father and to respect others as children of God.

Piety fosters obedience to God's commandments as expressions of His care for us and for our salvation. Piety engenders unshaken fidelity to God.

PRAYER. *Lord, You are indeed a God who cares for me.*

THE fear of the Lord is...destined to endure forever. —Ps 19:10

NOV. 27

...the Holy Spirit, the Lord...

REFLECTION. By the gift of the fear of the Lord, the Holy Spirit helps us see our proper relationship with God.

God is the infinite, immortal Creator; we are finite, mortal creatures. Far from making us tremble and cower before God, this gift enables us to stand in awe before God who stoops so low to love us.

PRAYER. *You are truly awesome, O God!*

HE Holy Spirit proceeds...from the communion of both the Father and the Son. —St. Augustine

NOV. 28

...who proceeds from the Father and the Son...

REFLECTION. In the mystery of the Trinity, each person gives Himself totally to the other.

The Father gives all that He is to the Son and the Son returns all to the Father and the bond of love between the two is the Holy Spirit.

PRAYER. *O God, You are a mystery of eternal life and love beyond my understanding.*

ORTHY are you, O Lord our God, to receive glory and honor... —Rev 4:11

NOV. 29

...who with the Father and the Son is adored and glorified...

REFLECTION. Since the Holy Spirit is God, we worship Him together with the Father and the Son, each equal in majesty, yet one God.

Adoring God, we praise Him for who He is. Glorifying God, we exalt His divine attributes and extol each person for their work in our redemption.

PRAYER. *Praise and glory to You, O most Holy Trinity!*

N PREVIOUS times, God spoke to our ancestors...through the Prophets... —Heb 1:1

NOV. 30

...who spoke through the prophets...

REFLECTION. The Father formed the Chosen People and prepared them for the coming of His only-begotten Son by raising up prophets inspired by the Holy Spirit to proclaim His message.

Through their words preserved in the Old Testament, the Holy Spirit still speaks God's eternal Word to us.

PRAYER. *Holy Spirit, open my ears to listen to God's Word and to accept it.*

HEN people spoke as messengers of God, they did so under the inspiration of the Holy Spirit. —2 Pet 1:21

DEC. 1

...who spoke through the prophets...

REFLECTION. At the child Jesus' presentation in the Temple, Simeon, filled with the Holy Spirit, and Anna the prophetess announced Jesus as the long-awaited Messiah (Lk 2:22, 28, 36-38).

At His baptism, John the Baptist, the last of the Old Testaments prophets, proclaimed Jesus the Messiah (Jn 1:29-34).

PRAYER. *Holy Spirit, help me point others to Jesus our Redeemer.*

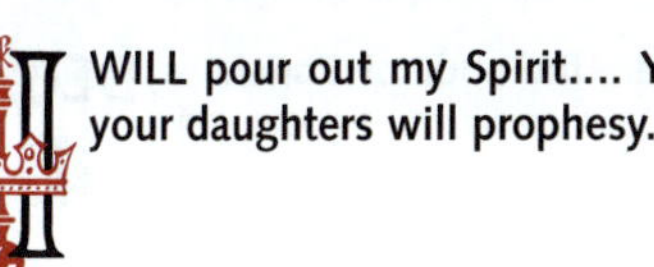

I WILL pour out my Spirit.... Your sons and your daughters will prophesy. —Joel 3:1

DEC. 2

...who spoke through the prophets...

REFLECTION. On Pentecost, the Holy Spirit poured out the gift of prophecy on the Church.

Acts of the Apostles numbers as prophets Barnabas, Agabus, Lucius, Manaen, Silas, Niger, Philip and his four daughters. Paul recognizes prophets as leaders of local communities. The prophets revealed God's will, encouraged believers, and led prayer.

PRAYER. *Holy Spirit, stir up in me Your gift of prophecy so I may proclaim Your Word.*

YOU are...a people claimed by God as his own possession... —1 Pet 2:9-10

DEC. 3

...in one, holy, catholic and apostolic Church...

REFLECTION. The word "Church" means "assembly." God assembled the Chosen People at Mt. Sinai to hear His Word and enter into covenant with Him.

Now He gathers us together in the Church as the People of God to hear His Word and to feed us with the Body of Christ.

PRAYER. *Lord, I thank You for making me a member of Your Church, the New Israel.*

YOU therefore are the body of Christ.
—1 Cor 12:27

DEC. 4

...in one, holy, catholic and apostolic Church...

REFLECTION. The Church is the Body of Christ. By baptism and the gift of the Holy Spirit, we are joined to Christ as living members of His Mystical Body.

Christ is the Head and each of us, united in one faith, contribute to the good of the whole Body with our diverse gifts.

PRAYER. *Lord, help me work with others for the good of the Church.*

ASK yourselves whether you belong to his flock,...whether the light of his truth shines in your minds.
—St. Gregory the Great

DEC. 5

...in one, holy, catholic and apostolic Church...

REFLECTION. The Church is the Flock of Christ. Jesus, the Good Shepherd, provides for us and protects us as His sheep.

As God led His people "like a flock by the hand of Moses and Aaron" (Ps 77:21), Jesus now guides us through the pastors He appoints over us.

PRAYER. *You, Lord, are my Good Shepherd.*

SO PRESENT yourselves...to such a bridegroom as a worthy bride. —St. Augustine

DEC. 6

...in one, holy, catholic and apostolic Church...

REFLECTION. The Church is the Bride of Christ. Jesus called Himself the bridegroom (Mk 2:19). As a husband becomes one flesh with his wife, Christ joins the Church to Himself and never stops loving her (Eph 5:21-32).

By the blood of the Cross, He washes her clean, sanctifying her and making her radiant with grace.

PRAYER. *Lord, grant me a faithful love of You.*

YOU are...God's building. —1 Cor 3:9

DEC. 7

...in one, holy, catholic and apostolic Church...

REFLECTION. When Peter confessed Jesus as "the Christ, the Son of the Living God" (Mt 16:16), Jesus promised to build His Church on Peter the rock.

This image of the Church as building reminds us that the Church is a visible reality, and we are called to build it by living our faith publicly and inviting others to join.

PRAYER. *Lord, may I never be ashamed of my faith and love of the Church.*

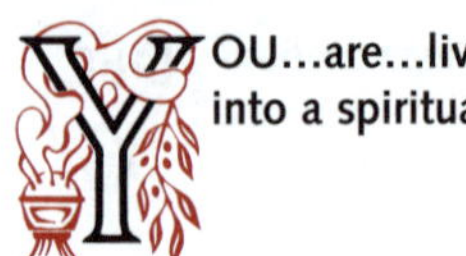

OU...are...living stones being built up into a spiritual temple... —1 Pet 2:5

DEC. 8

...in one, holy, catholic and apostolic Church...

REFLECTION. In Old Testament times, Israel's Temple was God's dwelling place.

By His Death and Resurrection, Christ made the Church the New Temple where God dwells. Furthermore, God dwells in every believer, making each believer's body "a temple of the Holy Spirit" (1 Cor 6:19).

PRAYER. *Lord, help me keep my body holy, and allow me to offer You fitting worship in the Church.*

E ARE God's coworkers... —1 Cor 3:9

DEC. 9

...in one, holy, catholic and apostolic Church...

REFLECTION. The prophet Isaiah spoke of Israel as the Lord's special vineyard (Isa 5:2-7).

Jesus used this image to speak of the Church as the vineyard taken from those who did not accept Him and given to those who did (Mt 20:1-8). The Church is God's vineyard. We are called to care for it, protect it, and work in it.

PRAYER. *Lord, help me always cherish Your Church.*

OU are...members of the household of God... —Eph 2:19

DEC. 10

...in one, holy, catholic and apostolic Church...

REFLECTION. Jesus taught us to pray to His Father as our Father (Mt 6:9), because all who do the will of His Father are His brothers and sisters and mother (Mt 12:50).

Gathered together as children of God, the Church, therefore, is God's family where we help one another grow in our love of God and neighbor.

PRAYER. *Lord, bless Your family with kindness and peace.*

OU are a chosen race, a royal priesthood... —1 Pet 2:9

DEC. 11

...in one, holy, catholic and apostolic Church...

REFLECTION. God chose Israel to be "a kingdom of priests" (Ex 19:6), offering Him worship and drawing other nations to Him.

The Church has inherited this identity as a priestly people. Baptized into Christ, we worship God "in Spirit and truth" (Jn 4:23) and draw others to praise and bless Him.

PRAYER. *Father, make my life a true sacrifice of praise to Your honor.*

THE sole Church of Christ,...one, holy, catholic, and apostolic...subsists in the Catholic Church...

—Lumen Gentium, 8

DEC. 12

...in one, holy, catholic and apostolic Church...

REFLECTION. These four characteristics belong to the Church that Jesus Himself founded and to her mission.

As the First Vatican Council taught, they are "a great and perpetual motive of credibility and an irrefutable witness of her divine mission" (*Dei Filius*, 3).

PRAYER. *Lord, help all people recognize the Church You founded for our salvation.*

I PRAY...May they all be one. As you, Father are in me and I in you, may they also be in us...

—Jn 17:20-21

DEC. 13

...in one, holy, catholic and apostolic Church...

REFLECTION. Just as the Father, the Son and the Holy Spirit are one, so also the Church, sharing in the life of God, is one.

Sent by the Father, the Risen Lord pours out the Holy Spirit to unite believers in faith, hope, and love.

PRAYER. *Father, safeguard the Church's unity.*

O NOT be afraid to be holy...since full, true freedom is born from holiness.

—Pope St. John Paul II

DEC. 14

...in one, holy, catholic and apostolic Church...

REFLECTION. As the Body of Christ, the Church shares fully in the holiness of Christ Himself.

By the power of the Holy Spirit, Christ sanctifies the Church, giving her "the fullness of means of salvation" (*Unitatis redintegratio* 3, 5). All her members, though imperfect, are called to live holy lives.

PRAYER. *Lord Jesus, may I treasure Your Church and my call to holiness.*

OD, our Savior...desires everyone to be saved and to come to full knowledge of the truth. **—1 Tim 2:4**

DEC. 15

...in one, holy, catholic and apostolic Church...

REFLECTION. The word "catholic" means "universal" or "all-inclusive." The Church is catholic because she includes all the baptized throughout the world.

Furthermore, the Church is catholic because the Risen Lord commanded her to "make disciples of all nations..." (Mt 28:19).

PRAYER. *Lord, lead all people to the Church You made the instrument of salvation.*

HE preaching of the truth...has been preserved in the Church from the apostles. —St. Irenaeus

DEC. 16

...in one, holy, catholic and apostolic Church...

REFLECTION. The Church is apostolic because Jesus established her on the foundation of the apostles. Guided by the Holy Spirit, the Church, faithfully and without error, hands on the faith that Jesus taught the apostles.

Furthermore, the Church is shepherded by the Pope and bishops who take the place of the apostles.

PRAYER. *Lord, keep me faithful to Your teaching.*

HE Church is...a sacrament of communion...grounded in the Trinitarian mystery of God... —Pope Benedict XVI

DEC. 17

...in one, holy, catholic and apostolic Church...

REFLECTION. The Church is not an international organization with local departments.

Every diocese is the Body of Christ in a particular place with all the means of salvation. United with the Pope and each other, local churches constitute the universal Church. Thus, the Church is a *communio*, a mystery of mutual sharing.

PRAYER. *Unite the Church in love, O Lord.*

HEAVEN is a city on a hill. Hence we cannot coast into it; we have to climb.

—Venerable Fulton Sheen

DEC. 18

...in one, holy, catholic and apostolic Church...

REFLECTION. The Church on earth is called the Church Militant, because her members struggle in a spiritual battle against the world, the flesh and the devil.

They endeavor to conquer sin in themselves and the world, thus transforming the world with God's love.

PRAYER. *Lord, keep me strong in my daily struggle against evil.*

THE purifying fires draw them ever upward and closer to God.

—St. Catherine of Genoa

DEC. 19

...in one, holy, catholic and apostolic Church...

REFLECTION. The faithful who have died without reaching perfect charity in this life undergo a purification in Purgatory before entering heaven.

They are called the Church Suffering. Their suffering is not the suffering of hell, but the pain of a burning desire to be with God who loves them so much.

PRAYER. *Eternal rest grant, O Lord, to the faithful departed.*

DO NOT weep, for I shall be more useful to you after my death and I shall help you... —St. Dominic

DEC. 20

...in one, holy, catholic and apostolic Church...

REFLECTION. Those who have died and gone to heaven are the Church Triumphant.

Freed from the imperfection and corruption of mortal life, they are celebrating Christ's victory over sin and death. They enjoy God's glory forever; and, by their prayers, they constantly intercede for us.

PRAYER. *All you holy saints of God, pray for me.*

BAPTISM is the "door" to faith and Christian life. —Pope Francis

DEC. 21

...I confess one Baptism for the forgiveness of sins...

REFLECTION. Baptism means "immersion." Immersed in the water, we die with Christ and are buried with Him.

We rise from the water, regenerated and made a new creature by Christ's Resurrection (Rom 6:2-4). Baptism is the first and fundamental sacrament that incorporates us into Christ, making us living members of the Church.

PRAYER. *Lord, renew within me the grace of my Baptism.*

APTISM is God's most beautiful...gift.... It is conferred on those who bring nothing of their own... —St. Gregory Nazianzen

DEC. 22

...I confess one Baptism for the forgiveness of sins...

REFLECTION. Baptism cleanses us of our sins. It washes away original sin inherited from Adam and all sins we have committed.

Even the punishment for our sins is forgiven. We are freed from the burden of the past to live a new life.

PRAYER. *Lord, thank You for the gift of Baptism and the grace of the sacrament!*

VERY baptized person...in the womb of the Church is transformed from a child of Adam to a child of God.

—St. Vincent Ferrer

DEC. 23

...I confess one Baptism for the forgiveness of sins...

REFLECTION. In Baptism, we are reborn "of water and the Spirit" (Jn 3:5).

We become the adopted children of God and "share in the divine nature" (2 Pet 1:4). We are made a "new creation" in Christ (2 Cor 5:17).

PRAYER. *Lord God, protect the new life You have given me as Your child.*

JESUS did not found several churches, but one single Church. —Pope St. John XXIII

DEC. 24

...I confess one Baptism for the forgiveness of sins...

REFLECTION. The sacrament of Baptism is administered only once because it effects a permanent change.

Once God claims us as His own, His choice remains. Furthermore, all who are properly baptized belong to Christ and His Church. Even baptized non-Catholics enjoy a certain but imperfect communion with the Church, because there is only one Baptism.

PRAYER. *Lord, gather Your Church as one.*

WHOEVER believes and is baptized will be saved... —Mk 16:16

DEC. 25

...I confess one Baptism for the forgiveness of sins...

REFLECTION. Before ascending to heaven, Jesus commanded the disciples to proclaim the gospel to all nations and to baptize them.

Baptism is necessary for salvation for those who hear the gospel and have the opportunity to receive this sacrament. We the baptized are called to help others believe in Jesus and receive Baptism.

PRAYER. *Lord, open the hearts of all to the Gospel.*

IT IS not his wish that any should perish... —2 Pet 3:9

DEC. 26

...I confess one Baptism for the forgiveness of sins...

REFLECTION. Although we are bound to the sacramental order, God is not.

God gives forgiveness of sins to those who die with the intention of receiving Baptism and to martyrs who shed their blood for the faith. Thus, besides baptism of water, there is baptism of blood and baptism of desire.

PRAYER. *Great, indeed, is Your mercy and love, O Lord!*

THE flesh shall rise again: certainly of every man, certainly the same flesh, and certainly in its entirety. —Tertullian

DEC. 27

...I look forward to the resurrection of the dead...

REFLECTION. Death entered the world by sin (Rom 5:12). Death separates our immortal soul from our mortal body.

At the end of the world, God will raise our bodies from the dust of the grave and unite them to our soul and make us whole again.

PRAYER. *Lord, You are the God of life.*

GOD, the wonderful and inexpressible Artisan, will...restore our flesh from the whole of the material of which it was constituted. —St. Augustine

DEC. 28

...I look forward to the resurrection of the dead...

REFLECTION. Christ's resurrected body is the pattern of our resurrection.

"He will transform our lowly bodies so that they will be conformed to his glorious body..." (Phil 3:21). Like the Risen Christ, we will be able to be seen, touched and heard.

PRAYER. *Lord, You have so wondrously created me for life.*

THE Host...implants...a seed of immortality, which one day must germinate. —Pope Leo XIII

DEC. 29

...I look forward to the resurrection of the dead...

REFLECTION. Jesus promised that those who eat His Body and drink His Blood He will raise up on the last day (Jn 6:54).

When we receive Jesus' glorified body in the Eucharist, we already have "the pledge of our bodily resurrection at the end of the world" (Pope St. John Paul II).

PRAYER. *Jesus, You are my hope and salvation.*

APPINESS in heaven is for those who know how to be happy on earth.

—St. Josemaria Escriva

DEC. 30

...and the life of the world to come.

REFLECTION. At the end of time, God will bring to completion His plan for creation.

He will transform creation into "a new heaven and a new earth" (Rev 21:1) where He dwells with us. Death will be no more, only life eternal and inexhaustible joy with God and each other.

PRAYER. *Lord, enliven my desire for heaven.*

HE future starts today, not tomorrow.

—Pope St. John Paul II

DEC. 31

...and the life of the world to come.

REFLECTION. Our desire for heaven does not lessen but only increases our work to order all things according to God's will.

Already through us, His Church, God is bringing together all things in Christ (Eph 1:10). The unity and love we foster among each other foreshadow and anticipate the age to come.

PRAYER. *May all I do, O God, be as You will.*

Act of Faith

FATHER, I praise and thank you for giving me the gift of faith in Jesus in Whom You have given us the fullness of Truth and Life.

I truly believe all that He has taught and done for our salvation.

Strengthen my faith as I face the trials of this life.

In Your mercy, let no doubt separate me from Your goodness.

Graciously enlighten my mind.

I pray, with Your Holy Spirit so that, firmly believing all that Christ has revealed and the Church teaches, I may practice what I believe so as to come to enjoy Your Love forever.

Bishop Serratelli

Prayer to Mary, Mother of the Church and Mother of Our Faith

Mother, help our faith!
Open our ears to hear God's word and to recognize his voice and call…

Help us to be touched by his love, that we may touch him in faith.

Help us to entrust ourselves fully to him and to believe in his love, especially at times of trial, beneath the shadow of the cross, when our faith is called to mature.

Sow in our faith the joy of the Risen One.

Remind us that those who believe are never alone.

Teach us to see all things with the eyes of Jesus, that he may be light for our path.

And may this light of faith always increase in us, until the dawn of that undying day which is Christ himself, your Son, our Lord!

Pope Francis

OTHER BOOKS BY THIS AUTHOR

EUCHARISTIC ADORATION: Scriptural Reflections and Prayers

The author's 21 meditations based on Scripture and packed with prayers and quotes from saints, popes, and more attest to the profound mystery and power of the Eucharist. 176 pages.

No. 947/19—Dura-Lux cover..... **11.95**

ISBN 978-1-953152-60-2

FROM THE CROSS TO THE EMPTY TOMB

The author invites you to journey with those who were with Jesus in His last hours. You may be like Peter one day, and like Judas, Simon, Mary Magdalene, or Our Lady on another. This Lenten book provides a deeper appreciation for God's eternal saving love. 96 pages.

No. 928/04—Flexible cover........... **7.95**

ISBN 978-1-947070-13-4

THE SEVEN GIFTS OF THE HOLY SPIRIT

Through history, art, Scripture, and Catholic documents, you will appreciate and grasp more fully how the seven gifts of the Holy Spirit can help you to live a truly authentic Christian life filled with peace and joy. 96 pages.

No. 930/04—Flexible cover **8.00**

ISBN 978-1-947070-23-3

ISBN 978-1-958237-85-4
90000
9 781958 237854